*To Anne, my wife of 52 years,*

*who left us too soon,*

*but is with us every day*

# CONTENTS

# WHERE DO I COME FROM?

This is for us fellas who are now Widowers and have never been involved with cooking during their married life because "she in the kitchen" supplied all that was needed.

Maybe you were allowed in the kitchen to bring a glass of wine while the miracle was being performed; or you helped with clearing up but not with a handle on what really went on there.

Women have more knowledge about cooking in their little fingers than I could acquire in two lifetimes – if that quickly!

Where I come from is a position where, when my wife was pregnant with our fourth said she could "Murder porridge" AND I did not know how. The best I could do was tea and toast (really very nice toast) in bed. She had seen this need for those of us of a certain age and without our spouses so she planned a course for delivery to U3A students in England.

I was the guinea pig. I cooked a meal from the course whilst she timed it; watched the difficulties in the process and refined until she had it sussed as they say. We were in Australia at the time and several of our friends were cajoled into being students whilst the whole course was practiced at home.

It soon became apparent that I could be useful on such a course making the meal she was demonstrating so she could then walk round the students looking at their work and assisting where necessary. (Rather like Fanny and Johnnie Craddock but without the evening dresses)

Producing a meal to entertain and make friends is an absolutely fabulous way of cementing those friendships and even making new ones - even if they come out of sheer curiosity!!!

You do have the memories so enjoy them even if few of your friends feel able to enter in – it really is a rich seam of encouragement. Your late spouse would prefer you found a way forward because sitting in a corner metaphorically wailing is of no help.

That is why I am doing this. It took me nearly 10 months before I started to cook despite having been part of her adventure of planning to teach cooking to gentlemen of my age group.

My son said why not start a blog and be positive. So I did. Not all the recipes on the blog are here but you can always refer to anymancancook.net for more recipes.

Having looked at Anne's recipe books I thought I could produce recipes in a way which we would find easier to follow so that explains the manner for the recipe layout – and I hope you will find them easy to follow.  There is no need to follow through from page one to the end – dip in as you feel moved - this is not a textbook and we are simply going to have fun doing what we probably have never done before.

For ease, I always suggest you buy what is readily available and not spend time making e.g. pastry. You can buy all types ready made and it does save time. If a celebrated cook like Delia Smith can write a book entitled "How to cheat at cooking" – we can 'cheat'!

The recipes are grouped together in both parts for similarity of taste, ease of making and just seem good together as, for example, in the Something Spectacular sections

Family and friends have piled in with support (the former probably because it is keeping me out of mischief). I do this for her and for me; actually us.

Tony Ashmore
December 2017

# PART ONE MAIN DISHES

**PIES**   Yes. Pies is where I am going to start because I found that once I had made a couple of pies handling ingredients seemed less threatening. Pies have a wide variety of content from meats such as beef, lamb, and chicken to fish to vegetables. The toppings can also vary quite widely from the more usual pastries; puff and short crust to mashed potatoes (including sweet potatoes) rosti and celeriac – what is that I hear you say but all will be revealed and you will like it.

The 'Larousse Gastronomique' (French book of all knowledge of cooking) points out that "Pies" was adopted from the English for "Magpie" – a bird famous for collecting items and hiding them in its nest. This reflects the idea that a mixture of ingredients can be combined under the pie crust or lid. (Now there's a Pub Quiz answer to store away!)

**HEARTY MEALS**     These are really good solid meals most of which need well over an hour to cook but are certainly worth waiting for.

**EASY**   these are mostly much quicker to cook than the Hearty meals and a couple of Vegetarian dishes as well. Especially Piedmont Peppers, which, we have eaten so frequently I can't count, and always satisfying. Also, here is the second fish recipe, which could just as easily be Haddock or Plaice although for me Cod works best.

**MEALS TO ENTERTAIN**     Well, of course, you can use any meal to entertain but these are both easy and interesting for any guest. The Moussaka especially works and the Harissa Lamb is an unusual recipe. So just go for it. Entertain your socks off.

**VEGETARIAN**      What shall I say about Vegetarian recipes? First, I have enjoyed vegetarian food over time, largely my eldest son's influence. Second, they taste really great. It really is only the timorous that shy away from such a good experience.

**SOMETHING SPECTACULAR and/or ADVENTUROUS**  These aren't quick or particularly easy but if you are up for trying to surprise and please guests these will blow their minds. Two of these need to be made overnight in some part and that makes them much easier, as there is no immediate pressure.

*Don't be frightened to experiment after you have tried a few of these recipes.*

# PIES

## Cottage or Shepherd's Pie

*Now this is the simplest meal to be found here or on my blog. That does not in any way reduce its goodness and usefulness. I always have one or two in my freezer in case of an emergency; unexpected guest or simply can't be bothered with real cooking today (occasionally being lazy is allowed). If you want to make the mash yourself the method is at the bottom.*

**INGREDIENTS**

| 500 g | Minced Beef for Cottage pie | Minced Lamb if Shepherd's Pie |
|---|---|---|
| 1 | Small Onion | Chopped very small |
| 2 cubes | Beef or Lamb stock | Depending on the meat you are using |
| 500 ml | Boiling water | To prepare the Stock |
| 100 g | Instant Mash ('Smash') | |
| 40 g | Grated Cheese | You can buy this – saves work |

**METHOD**
**PRE-HEAT OVEN** 220ºC Fan
**PLACE** Mince in a deep saucepan
**ADD** Prepared Stock
**COVER** with more water so Mince is completely covered
**ADD** Chopped Onion
**BRING** to boil then **TURN DOWN HEAT**
**SIMMER** for1hour
**REMOVE** from saucepan and transfer to oven dish with a slotted spoon to avoid too much liquid going over
**MAKE** up Instant Mash per packet instructions
**COVER** Mince mixture with the Instant Mash
**SMOOTH** the surface
**COVER** with the Cheese
**BAKE** in middle of oven for 15 minutes till the cheese melts and goes golden

*If you prefer to make your own Mash here's how: -*
*Using 300 g potatoes; peel and cover with water in a good-sized pan. Bring to boil and simmer for up to 15 minutes – until potatoes are tender. Drain and mash potatoes with a knob of butter until smooth. Then cover the mixture as before.*

# Shepherd's Pie with a twist

*Slightly more work for this one but very worthwhile. It involves slow cooking of a shoulder joint of Lamb. This can be cooked overnight and is best, because it needs some 8 hours at least. You will be surprised at how different this tastes from buying ready-made mince.*

## INGREDIENTS

| | | |
|---|---|---|
| 1 | Shoulder of Lamb | On the bone |
| 6 | Large Baking Potatoes | |
| 100 ml | Double Cream | |
| 100 g | Butter | |
| 6 | Egg Yolks | |
| 1 | Large Onion | Peeled and diced |
| 2 | Carrots | Peeled and diced |
| 1 | Celery Stalk | Diced |
| 8 | Garlic Cloves | Chopped finely |
| 500 ml | Chicken Stock | |
| Sprig | Rosemary | Chopped finely |
| 4 Sprigs | Thyme | |
| 3 tbsp | Worcestershire Sauce | |
| 3 tbsp | Tomato Puree | |
| 3 tbsp | Oil | |
| Pinch | Salt & Pepper | Season to taste |

**METHOD**

**PLACE** Shoulder of Lamb on a wire rack on a roasting tray

**COVER** loosely with foil

**SLOW ROAST** at 170ºC at least 8 hours or overnight

**REMOVE** all the meat and discard all fat and skin. (Do this whilst warm)

**SHRED** meat into bite-sized pieces

**WRAP** the Potatoes in foil and

**BAKE** for an hour at 200ºC

**PUT** aside until cool enough to handle

**MEANTIME**

**HEAT THE** Oil in a pan then

**ADD** Onion, Carrots and Celery **COOK** until soft

**STIR** in Tomato Puree, Worcestershire Sauce and the Lamb **MIX** well

**POUR** in Chicken Stock **SIMMER** for about 20 minutes

**SCOOP** out the potato flesh into a separate pan

**BRING** Butter and Double Cream to the boil **BEAT** into the Potatoes

**MIX** in the 6 egg yolks

**PUT** Lamb into a casserole dish

**SPREAD** the Potato mix over the Lamb

**PLACE** in an oven pre-heated to 180ºC **COOK** 20 mins or until golden

# Celeriac Cottage Pie

*Here's a cottage pie that is different, mainly because the usual topping of potato is exchanged for Celeriac. This is a root vegetable of the same family as Celery but it's not interchangeable. There will be fewer calories than if potato is used. Mind you I don't usually bother about calorie counting just have modest helpings of whatever you eat.*

## INGREDIENTS

| | | |
|---|---|---|
| 250 g | Minced Beef | Best quality you can find |
| 500 g | Celeriac | Peeled and cubed |
| 100 g | Low fat Crème Fraiche | |
| 400 g | Tin Chopped Tomatoes | |
| 2 | Leeks | Trimmed and sliced thinly |
| 1 | Large Onion | Diced |
| 2 | Carrots | Peeled & Diced |
| 2 | Celery Stalks | Finely Chopped |
| 2 tbsp | Tomato Puree | |
| 1 tbsp | Worcestershire Sauce | |
| 2 | Bay leaves | |
| 1 tsp | Thyme leaves | Chopped |
| 300 ml | Boiling Water | |
| 2 | Oxo Cubes | |
| 1 tsp | Groundnut Oil | |
| | Spraying Oil | |
| | Salt & Pepper to taste | |

**METHOD**
**SPRAY** a large pan with the Oil
**BROWN** the Minced Beef
**ADD** Onion, Carrot and Celery for about 10 minutes
**STIR** in the Chopped Tomatoes, Tomato Puree, Bay Leaves, Thyme, Worcestershire Sauce, Oxo Cubes and the Water
**BOIL** then
**COVER** and simmer for 30 minutes.
**STIR** occasionally
**MEANTIME**
**BOIL** Celeriac Cubes until tender
**DRAIN & MASH** with the Crème Fraiche to a coarseness you prefer
**PRE-HEAT** Oven 200°C
**HEAT** Groundnut Oil in a pan and
**SAUTE** the Leeks
**ADD** to the mashed Celeriac and season to taste
**PLACE** Minced beef in an ovenproof dish
**POUR** the Celeriac mixture over the top
**BAKE** for 25 – 30 minutes until golden on top
**SERVE** with Green vegetables, Broccoli, or Peas or Cabbage etc.

## Chicken Pie topped with Rosti

*This can be made ahead of actual requirements leaving only the baking to go ahead. You have two choices for the chicken. Either buy ready-diced chicken – but be careful not to have too large segments. Otherwise buy two skinless chicken breasts and dice them yourself.*
*As for the Rosti whilst it is easy to make it is even easier to buy*

### INGREDIENTS

| 300 g | Chicken | Diced |
|---|---|---|
| 200 g | Ready made Rosti | Most supermarkets |
| 100 g | Broccoli Spears | Cut into 2.5 cm lengths |
| 1 | Onion | Thinly sliced |
| 200 g | Crème Fraiche | |
| 1 tbsp | Olive Oil | |
| 1 tbsp | Wholegrain Mustard | |
| 15 g | Tarragon | Finely Chopped |

### METHOD
**PRE-HEAT** oven to 190ºC fan
**PLUNGE** Broccoli into boiling water for 2 mins (known as Blanching)
**DRAIN** and set aside for the moment
**HEAT** the Oil in a medium saucepan
**COOK** the Onion for 3-4 minutes till softened and golden
**MEANWHILE**
**STIR** the Crème Fraiche & Mustard into the saucepan and **SIMMER**
**ADD** the Chicken and continue **SIMMERING** for 5 minutes
**ADD** Broccoli & Tarragon
**POUR** the mixture into a baking dish
**CRUMBLE** the Rosti over the top
**BAKE** for 20 – 25 minutes until golden and bubbling
**SERVE** with Carrots as that gives colour.

## Leek Pie

*This is a Vegetarian Dish but is easy and tasteful and also freezes well. My vegetarian son likes it a lot.*

**INGREDIENTS**

| 5 | Leeks | Trimmed, halved horizontally, sliced 5cm, washed and shaken dry |
|---|---|---|
| 75 g | Butter | |
| ¼ tsp | Ground Nutmeg | |
| 100 ml | Double Cream | |
| 2 x 320 g | Rolls Puff Pastry | Chilled or Frozen – if frozen it will need a couple of hours to thaw enough to work |
| 1 | Egg | Beaten |
| Pinch | Salt and Pepper | Season to taste |

**METHOD**

**PRE-HEAT** oven 180ºC fan

**MELT** the butter in a large frying pan

**ADD** leeks and

**COOK** over a low heat for 10 – 15 minutes stirring frequently as they will quite quickly start to turn brown.

**MIX** Double Cream, nutmeg, salt and pepper then

**ADD** to leeks

**INCREASE** heat slightly and allow mixture to "reduce" a little. Another time for watching carefully for signs of burning, stirring helps prevent this.

**TURN** the mixture onto a clean plate to cool, meanwhile

**PLACE** one of the Pastry sheets onto a floured surface and cut a circle 18 cm in diameter

**PLACE** the circle onto a baking tray lined with baking parchment

**USE** the second Pastry sheet to cut a circle of 20 cm diameter. You may need to roll the sheet out a little to achieve the right size

**BRUSH** a 2.5 cm margin all-round the edge of the smaller circle with the beaten egg

**SPOON** the leek mixture onto the smaller pastry circle

**LIFT** second pastry circle onto the smaller carefully matching the edges and sealing them with pressure from a fork all way round

**BRUSH** pie all over with remainder of beaten egg

**MAKE** a stem vent in the middle

**BAKE** for 20 -25 mins or until pie turns golden.

# Spring Vegetable & Chicken Pie

*The basis for this came from another food site renbenham.com and I thought it was good. I made it and it is. I've varied it a little and taken out the carrots (needed for colour when serving) and added sliced mushrooms. You will like it and it impresses guests!!*

## INGREDIENTS

| 1 tsp | Rapeseed oil | Or Olive Oil |
|---|---|---|
| 1 | Onion | Peeled & Chopped |
| I | Stick of Celery | Chopped |
| 700 g | Chicken Breasts | Chopped |
| 25 g | Sliced Mushrooms | Come in a tin |
| 2 | Courgettes | Cubed but not too large |
| 200 g | Asparagus | Chopped |
| 200 g | Crème Fraiche | |
| 1 | Packet ready rolled puff pastry | Size about 315/325g need to let it thaw for about 2/3hours |
| 1 tbsp | Flour | |
| 1 tbsp | Butter | |
| 1 | Egg | Beaten |
| Sprinkling | Salt and pepper | |

## METHOD
**PREHEAT** the oven to 180°C
**HEAT** Oil in a large frying pan – the biggest you've got
**ADD** Onions, Celery and fry for 5 minutes – keep stirring all the time
**ADD** Chicken and fry for 7 minutes – keep stirring as before
**ADD** Courgettes, Asparagus, Mushrooms and fry for a further 3 minutes
**STIR** in the Crème Fraiche and season with salt & pepper
**TRANSFER** the mixture to the pie dish
**UNROLL** the pastry onto a clean, floured surface
**BUTTER** the rim of the pie dish
**LIFT** the pastry over the top of the pie dish. You might need to roll it out a little to ensure a fit
**PRESS** the edges down gently with a fork
**TRIM** excess pastry
**BRUSH** the pastry all over with the beaten egg
**BAKE** for 30 minutes or until puffed up and golden colour

## Fish & Prawn Pie

*Now this is a good fish recipe, which, started as one of Waitrose's but has been adapted to my tastes. It can be cooked with either Cod or Haddock. It's quick to prepare and there are a number of choices depending on your preferences. Are you into Sweet Potatoes or more ordinary? Do you like Jumbo Prawns or the smaller more delicate ones – the latter are my preference? Again, it is as good with Cod or Haddock. Just sit back and have a drink as it cooks.*

**INGREDIENTS**

| | | |
|---|---|---|
| 750 g | Potatoes | Maris Piper or Sweet Potatoes |
| 30 g | Butter | You'll need an extra knob |
| 30 g | Plain Flour | |
| 400 ml | Full Fat Milk | Not semi or wholly skimmed |
| 400 g | Haddock (skinless) or Cod | Cut into large chunks |
| 180 g | Prawns | Jumbo or smaller sized prawns |
| 150 g | Petits Pois | |
| 150 g | Cheese Cheddar or your preference | Coarsely grated |
| 1 tsp | Dijon Mustard | |
| 25 g | Chives | Finely chopped |

**METHOD**
**PRE-HEAT** Oven 200ºC fan
**PLACE** Potatoes in a good-sized pan
**COVER** with water and bring to
**BOIL** and
**SIMMER** for 10/15 minutes till Potatoes are tender
**MEANTIME** Melt the Butter in another saucepan.
**ADD** Flour and cook for 2 minutes
**BEAT** in Milk gradually
**BRING** to boil and
**SIMMER** for 2/3 minutes until thickened
**REMOVE** from heat and stir in the Fish, Petits Pois and about ¾ of the Cheese, Mustard and the Chives
**SPOON** into cooking dish
**DRAIN & MASH** Potatoes until smooth
**BEAT** in the knob of Butter and Milk
**SPOON** over the Fish
**SCATTER** over the balance of the Cheese
**SEASON** to taste and
**BAKE** 30 mins until pie is bubbling and golden.
**SERVE** with green vegetables i.e. Broccoli; Asparagus or Courgettes. Or of course Carrots

## Steak, Mushroom & Ale Pie

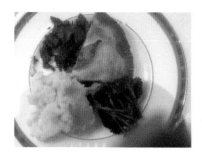

*This is another of those recipes of which part can be performed well before the final stages i.e. overnight or even up to a couple of days in the freezer. It does make entertaining easier since you only have to bake the pie on the day. But do remember to defrost the pastry well before using. Again, Waitrose in England provided the basic recipe. As usual this will make enough for 4 so at least two for the freezer. You might find when using the frozen portions that additional gravy might be needed, as the freezing process tends to dry up the moisture. Cooks outside England may have to search for suitable dark brown ale because 'Old Peculiar' is indeed peculiar to English shores.*

### INGREDIENTS

| | | |
|---|---|---|
| 400 g | Diced Braising Steak | |
| 1 | Large Onion | Well chopped |
| 3 | Rashers Streaky Back Bacon | Roughly chopped |
| 2 tbsp | Vegetable Oil | |
| 4 tbsp | Plain Flour | Plus extra for dusting |
| 150 ml | Theakston Old Peculiar | |
| 200 ml | Beef Stock | |
| 2 tsp | Muscavado Sugar | Light brown |
| Bunch | Thyme or Rosemary | |
| 2 | Carrots | Cut into chunks |
| 100 g | Button Mushrooms | Thinly sliced |
| 400 g | Short crust Pastry | |
| | A little Milk | For brushing |

## METHOD

**HEAT** ½ the Oil in a large saucepan with a tight-fitting lid or a large heavy-bottomed frying pan also with a lid. I prefer the latter.

**COOK** the Diced Steak until browned. Depending on the size of the 'dices' can take from 3 – 5 minutes but watch it all the time so as not to let it burn (it did for me first time I made it!!)

**REMOVE** when cooked using a slotted spoon and set aside

**ADD** Flour to the pan cooking for about a minute

**STIR** in the Ale scraping up any bits stuck to the bottom of the pan

**ADD** Stock, Sugar, Herbs, Carrots and Meat

**COVER** with lid and gently simmer for up to two hours, at least until the meat is tender

***This is the point where you can let the mixture cool and chill in the fridge or even freeze.***

***Continue as follows: -***

**PRE-HEAT** oven to 220ºC fan

**STIR** Mushrooms into the mixture then

**TRANSFER** mixture into a 20 cm pie dish

**ROLL OUT** the Pastry on a lightly floured surface

**DAMPEN** the rim of the pie dish

**PLACE** Pastry over the dish

**TRIM** the edges and press down well

**MAKE** a hole in the centre as a vent

**BRUSH** all over with the milk

**BAKE** for 30 minutes or until the pastry is golden

**SERVE** with mashed potato and a green vegetable.

# HEARTY MEALS

## Murphy Casserole

*Here is another family favourite from the past. The children seemingly could not get enough of this. It is simple but it is best when you cook the ham yourself and the method for this is shown in the Techniques section.*

**INGREDIENTS**

| 5/6 | Large Potatoes | Thinly sliced |
|---|---|---|
| 600 g | Cooked ham | Thinly sliced See Ham in Cider in Techniques section |
| 4 | Leeks<br>Or<br>2 large onions | Washed and sliced<br>Or<br>Sliced and chopped |
| 1 | Can Condensed Chicken Soup | Made according to instructions |

**METHOD**
**PLACE** Potatoes in saucepan
**COVER** with boiling water
**BRING** back to boil for 2 mins
> *This is the treacherous stage, if you don't watch like a hawk they will cook too much and fall to pieces*

**DRAIN** and cover with cold water to halt further cooking
**STARTING** and **ENDING** with potatoes
**LAYER** Potatoes, Ham and Leeks (or Onions) in casserole dish
**POUR** over the prepared soup.
**COOK** for about 1½ hours in a medium Oven say about 150-160ºC fan. It is     very difficult to be precise as it depends on the Potatoes, which can vary
a great deal
**CHECK** after 1 hour. If Potatoes are nice and tender the casserole is done otherwise continue cooking.

# Tomato, Chicken, Rosemary & Mashed Potatoes

*I know the title is almost longer than the list of ingredients but it is simple and very tasty*

## INGREDIENTS

| | | |
|---|---|---|
| 4 | Rashers Streaky Bacon | Sliced into small strips |
| 1 | Large Onion | Halved and sliced thinly |
| 1 | Celery Heart | Rinsed, Sliced, root discarded |
| 6 | Small Carrots | Peeled & trimmed |
| 2 | Chicken Breasts | Drumsticks or thighs are OK |
| 3 tbsp | Vegetable Oil | |
| 2 | Sweet Potatoes | Washed & peeled |
| 3 stalks | Rosemary | Strip the leaves off |
| 1/2 Cup | Cream | Single or Double |
| 25 g | Butter | For creaming potatoes |
| 4 cloves | Garlic | Crushed |
| 1 tbsp | Plain Flour | |
| 1 glass | Wine Red or White | White probably better |
| 250 ml | Creamed Tomato | Chopped Toms in Processor |
| 2 tbsp | Flat Leafed Parsley | Finely Chopped |
| Pinch | Salt & Pepper to taste | |

## METHOD

**FRY** Bacon crisp in a heavy bottomed pan
**REMOVE** Bacon and set aside
**ADD** Onion, Celery and Rosemary to pan
**SEASON** as required
**COVER** and
**COOK** gently for 10 mins so vegetables wilt but not change colour
**STIR** occasionally
**REMOVE** to a plate
**CUT** the Chicken into 3 cm cubes or nuggets
**DUST** the Chicken in the flour coating all sides
**ADD** more oil and **COOK** the Chicken until golden all over
**POUR** in Wine stirring to make a smooth sauce
**ADD** Tomato stirring as it comes up to simmer
**NOW ADD** Onion, Celery and Carrots
**SIMMER** gently for 30 minutes so Chicken and Carrots are tender
**STIR** in Bacon and Parsley just before serving.
**BOIL** the Sweet potatoes and when soft
**MASH** together with Butter, Cream, Garlic and a dash more pepper
***CAREFUL WHEN SERVING TO HAVE JUST ENOUGH OF THE LIQUID WITHOUT WASHING AWAY THE MASHED POTATO***

## Lamb & Beans

*Doesn't sound exciting but I have not "invented" a better name, despite that, it truly is a "superb" meal (which is what my late wife wrote on the recipe when she first made this in 2000)*
*Having found it and recently made it I confirm her description.*
*Oh, and it freezes very well.*

### INGREDIENTS

| | | |
|---|---|---|
| 400 g | Diced Lamb | Shanks or shoulder |
| 2 | Red Onions | Thinly sliced |
| 6 | Garlic cloves | Chopped |
| 1 can | Chopped Tomatoes | About 400 g |
| 1 can | Flageolet Beans | Ditto |
| 2 glasses | Red Wine | |
| 2 | Bay Leaves | |
| 2 tbsp | Thyme | Add whilst cooking |
| 2 tbsp | Flat Leaf Parsley | Add when serving |

### METHOD
**CHOOSE** a large saucepan
**PLACE** Onions, Garlic, Beans, Tomatoes, Wine, Bay Leaves and Thyme in saucepan and
**BRING TO BOIL** when bubbling
**ADD** Diced Lamb
**TURN** Lamb well into the mixture until it is brought back to boil
**REDUCE** Heat and simmer on top of the stove or in oven at 150ºC
**COOK** for approx. 2 hours
**CHECK** at 1½ hours to see if meat is tender

## Beef & Potato Casserole

*This is an excellent meal for a cold wet day. When I first made this, I used red wine but that coloured the whole meal so I now only use white wine and it leaves a meal worthy of photographing*

### INGREDIENTS

| | | |
|---|---|---|
| 500 g | Topside Steak | Cut into 1 inch cubes |
| 250 g | Potatoes | Sliced thinly |
| 2 | Bacon Rashers | Cut into small cubes |
| 1 | Onion | Peel and quarter |
| 60 g | Butter | Need extra for dotting |
| 1 tbsp | Virgin Oil | |
| 1 ½ Cups | Water | |
| 1 | Beef Stock Cube | Crumbled |
| ½ Cup | White Wine | See comment above about Red Wine |
| 2 tsp | Tomato Paste | |
| 2 tbsp | Plain Flour | |
| 2 tsps | Dijon Mustard | |
| 15 g | Butter | |

### METHOD
**HEAT** Butter and Oil in a pan
**ADD** Meat little at a time ensure brown on all sides
**REMOVE** Meat to a plate
**ADD** Onion and Bacon to the pan
**COOK** for 3 minutes
**REMOVE** Onion and Bacon
**STIR** in Flour cook for 1 minute
**ADD** Water, Crumbled Stock Cube, Wine, and Tomato Paste & Mustard to make the sauce
**MIX** well
**STIR** until boiling; **REDUCE** heat and **SIMMER** for 5 minutes
**PLACE** Meat, Onion & Bacon mixture into casserole dish
**POUR** sauce over
**LAYER** Potato Slices on top
**DOT** with extra Butter
**COVER and BAKE** at 160ºC for 1¼ hours.
**DURING** last 20 minutes remove cover so Potatoes brown nicely

# Bean & Pepper Hotpot

*This is a leisurely vegetarian meal to make. I know some of you out there think that a vegetarian meal cannot be very good. Come on you are old enough to know better. The ingredients come out in full flavour if made a few days in advance of requirements.  This makes 4 servings and because you can use it one helping at a time with, for example, a salmon fillet (which I did just yesterday to get a taste), before serving it in a couple of days' time. Chicken would also work I think.  Also good is the possibility of using a range of beans beyond the two I am now using. However, we are to finish this off with rice. So here goes*

## INGREDIENTS

| 100 ml | Extra Virgin Olive Oil | |
|---|---|---|
| 2 | Red Peppers | Seeds removed then sliced |
| 2 | Medium Onions | Thinly sliced |
| 2 | Leeks | Sliced into 2 cm pieces |
| 3 | Sticks Celery | Finely sliced |
| 2 | Carrots | Finely diced |
| 2 | Red Chilies | Sliced diagonally seeds left in |
| 4 | Garlic cloves | Sliced |
| 1 tsp | Paprika | |
| 1 tbsp | Fennel Seeds | |
| 2 tsps | Thyme | Fresh or dried |
| 800 g | Red Kidney Beans about 2 tins | Drained and rinsed |
| 800 g | Haricot Beans about 2 tins | Ditto |
| 400 g | Chopped Tomatoes | Tinned |
| 1 Cup | Rice for each two servings | |
| | Salt & Pepper | For seasoning to taste |

## METHOD

**COOK** Peppers & Chilies in the Olive Oil over a medium heat for about 6 minutes.

**DO USE** a large saucepan as every ingredient goes in.

**ADD** Carrot, Celery, Leek, Garlic, Onion and Thyme

**COOK** for up to 15 minutes until the mixture appears caramelised.

**ADD** Kidney and Haricot Beans (or whatever it is you are using)

**SEASON** with Salt & Pepper

**ADD** Chopped Tomatoes

**STIR** through

**ADD** Just enough water to cover and

**SIMMER** on a low heat for 30 mins.

***This is where you can stop and leave the mixture, covered, till you are ready to reheat and serve. It will marinate nicely whilst waiting***

**PRE-HEAT OVEN** to 200ºC fan

**PLACE IN OVEN** for 15 mins but test it is warmed right through at 10 mins. Using a microwave about 3 mins for each 2 tablespoons of hotpot serving.

**PREPARE** Rice as in the Techniques section or buy a ready cooked rice such as Uncle Bens or similar – it usually only needs 90 seconds.

**SPOON** Hotpot over rice

## Spiced Pork with Apricots

*Extremely good from Betty Crowle, the ingredients below are sufficient for 4 servings. If halving the number of pork steaks use only 1 onion and reduce the amount of apricots and vegetable stock. As for the rest, I would leave the same – but if you want to be precise do the same for the rest*

**INGREDIENTS**

| | | |
|---|---|---|
| 4 | Pork Loin Steaks | Trim fat off |
| 3 tbsp | Seasoned Flour | Plain flour with salt & pepper |
| 3 tbsp | Olive oil | For steaks and onions |
| 2 | Large Onions | Sliced but not too finely |
| 1 tbsp | Granulated Sugar | |
| ½ tsp | Ground Allspice | |
| ½ tsp | Ground Cinnamon | |
| 2 tbsp | Red Wine Vinegar | |
| 10 g | Dried ready to eat apricots | Snipped into strips |
| 250 ml | Vegetable stock | 1 stock cube |

**METHOD**
**PREHEAT** oven to 170°C fan
**COAT** the Pork with seasoned Flour. (Put Flour into a plastic bag and drop Pork in and shake about).
**FRY** until brown then place in casserole dish
**CLEAN** the pan and
**FRY** the Onions until beginning to brown
**ADD** Sugar; continue frying until Onions caramelize (e.g. turn a deep golden colour–this may take longer than expected - quite a few minutes)
**STIR** in Spices, Vinegar and 2 tablespoons of water
**SIMMER** and continue until syrupy.
**ADD** Stock and Apricots
**POUR** over Pork.
**COVER** with tinfoil
**COOK** for 1½ hours or until the Pork is tender – check after one hour

**Goes very well with green vegetables and boiled new potatoes –absolutely delicious!**

# EASY

## Smoked Salmon & Asparagus Flan

*This is really useful because it is good cooked and eaten or frozen till the appropriate moment. I do not apologise for commenting about cooking for entertaining. Our other, now departed, halves would expect it; flopping around with no direction is NO direction at all! So, let's move it....*

**INGREDIENTS**

| 1 sheet | Ready-rolled Short Crust Pastry | |
|---|---|---|
| 150 g | Smoked Salmon pieces | |
| Tin | Asparagus | Or 350 g fresh, trimmed & lightly cooked |
| 3 | Eggs | |
| 250 ml | Single Cream | Or Half-and-half |
| ¼ tsp | Black Pepper | Freshly ground |
| 50 g | Cheddar Cheese | Grated |
| 75 g | Fresh Breadcrumbs | White bread is best here |
| ½ tsp | Paprika | |

**METHOD**
**ROLL** Pastry into a disc measuring 2½ cm larger than flan dish you propose using
**LINE** dish with the pastry
**BEAT** Eggs & Cream together and season with Pepper
**COMBINE** Cheese & Breadcrumbs in a separate bowl
**ARRANGE** Uncooked Salmon and Asparagus into pastry case
**POUR** Egg and Cream mixture over Salmon & Asparagus
**SPRINKLE** Cheese & Breadcrumbs mixture evenly over Salmon and Asparagus
**BAKE** on 170$^0$C fan for 35 – 40 min until puffed up and golden,

**Freezes well**

# Herbed Cod

*This is a nice supper dish for two and is a derivative of another Waitrose recipe.*

## INGREDIENTS

| 2 x 150 g | Cod Fillets | |
|-----------|-------------|---|
| 1 sprig | Fresh Rosemary | Leaves removed from stem and finely chopped |
| 20 g | Fresh Flat Leafed Parsley | Finely chopped |
| 25 g | White Breadcrumbs | These can be bought but so much better of you do it yourself in the Food Processor |
| 1 | Lemon for the juice | |
| 1 can | Lentils about 400 g | Rinsed and drained |
| 6 | Spring/salad Onions | |
| 2 tsp | Balsamic Glaze | |

## METHOD
**PRE-Heat** oven to 200ºC fan
**PLACE** Cod in a baking dish
**MIX** Herbs, Breadcrumbs and Lemon juice together
**PRESS** on top of the fillets
**COVER** with foil and
**BAKE** for 10 minutes
**REMOVE** foil and cook for 5 more minutes until Breadcrumbs turn golden
**WHILE** that is happening
**MIX** the Lentils with the Onions and Balsamic Glaze
**PLACE** the Lentils onto two serving plates and
**TOP** with the Cod Fillets
**SERVE** with New Potatoes and/or Roasted Vine Tomatoes

# Chicken Risotto

*You will need to think about vegetables to serve with this. I suggest that you serve some or all of these – carrots, broccoli, leeks and courgettes to give the dish some colour. Steaming them is best. (Remember root vegetables in the bottom of the saucepan in the water with the rest in the steamer vessel above). This will make enough for four so maybe two are destined for freezer. BUT do remember what is in the freezer and use it otherwise as Terry Wogan said "the freezer becomes the Bermuda Triangle"*

## INGREDIENTS

| 500 g | Chicken (probably 3 breasts) | Cut into bite size pieces |
|---|---|---|
| | Flour | Enough to lightly dust chicken |
| 2 tbsp | Olive Oil | |
| 30 g | Butter | |
| 1 | Onion | Peeled and chopped |
| 30 g | Sliced Mushrooms | |
| 1 cup | Rice – Risotto preferred | Or Long Grain |
| 3 cups | Water | |
| 1 | Chicken Stock Cube | Crumbled |
| | Salt & Pepper | Pinches of each |

## METHOD

**HEAT** Butter and Oil in a large frying pan

**ADD** Chicken and brown well.  Need to keep turning it to prevent one side becoming burnt

**REMOVE** from pan and put on plate covered with kitchen paper

**ADD** to the pan chopped Onion and cook until transparent but not burnt

**ADD** Rice

**COOK** stirring for 2 minutes

**ADD** Water and Crumbled Stock Cube

**BRING** to boil

**REDUCE** heat and now **ADD** Chicken

**SIMMER** covered for 30 minutes

*Don't forget to steam the vegetables about 10 – 15 mins before end of Risotto cooking time.*

# Pork Chops & Apples

*This is a natural combination. It is easy to prepare and tastes good. Timing is critical as unlike some of my recipes you need to be at the Hob for most of the time. But I bet your guests will be happy to hang around; chat and enjoy a glass of Prosecco while you bring this to the point of serving.*

### INGREDIENTS

| | | |
|---|---|---|
| 1 tbsp | Olive Oil | |
| 1 | Cox's Orange Pippin | Or Pink Lady; cored and sliced |
| 2 | Pork Chops | About 200 g each |
| 150 ml | Dry Cider | |
| 100 ml | Crème Fraiche | |
| 2 | Sprigs Fresh Sage | |
| 1 tbsp | Redcurrant Jelly | |
| | Salt & Pepper | Freshly ground |

### METHOD

**HEAT** Olive Oil in a large non-stick frying pan
**COOK** Apples for 3-4 minutes on either side until golden brown
**SET ASIDE** on a plate to wait for right moment
**SEASON** Chops with Pepper & Salt and
**ADD** to the frying pan
**COOK** for about 5 minutes turning until golden brown
**ADD** Sage and Cider
**SIMMER** for say 15 minutes so chops are really cooked
**TRANSFER** Chops to a separate plate and
**COVER** with foil and rest for a few minutes
**STIR** Redcurrant Jelly into frying pan
**SIMMER** for a few minutes to allow jelly to dissolve
**STIR** in Crème Fraiche and Apples
**HEAT** through and season to taste
**SPOON** Apples over Chops and
**SERVE**

## Easy Salmon Dinner

*Just got switched into fish recipes and there are a couple further on. As a starter, this worked for my intrepid tester and me. It's a quick easy dish and very satisfying. Just try it and see.*

**INGREDIENTS**

| 2 | Boneless Salmon Filets | |
|---|---|---|
| 200 g | Carrots | Peeled and sliced |
| 200 g | Broccoli | |
| 2 tbsp | Olive Oil | |
| 2 tsp | Black Pepper | Freshly Ground |
| 100 g | Brown Sugar | |
| 4 tbsp | Soy Sauce | |
| 40 g | Honey | |
| 2 tbsp | Sesame Seeds | |
| | Salt & Pepper | To taste |

**METHOD**
**PRE HEAT** oven to 200ºC
**COMBINE** on a baking sheet Carrots, Broccoli, Oil, and Salt & Pepper
**MAKE** sure all vegetables are coated
**ARRANGE** in the centre of the sheet
**LAY** Salmon Fillets on the vegetables
**COMBINE** Brown Sugar, Soy Sauce, Honey, and Sesame Seeds
**MIX** until smooth
**SPREAD** over top of Salmon
**BAKE** for 12 minutes
**REMOVE** Salmon Fillets from the vegetables and set aside
**TOSS** the vegetables in the roasting juices
**GLAZE** the Salmon with any juice remaining
**SERVE**

# Piedmont Peppers

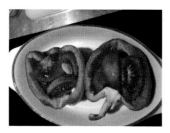

*This has been a favourite since Betty gave us the recipe and I think you may like it too It is easy; light on calories and useful for a lunch or light evening meal. Although Anchovies are part of the meal I never use them, as there is good taste without*

## INGREDIENTS

| 2 | Large Red Peppers | Halved and deseeded |
|---|---|---|
| 3 | Large Tomatoes | Peeled (see below) |
| 4 | Cloves Garlic | Finely sliced |
| 12 ml | Olive or Vegetable Oil | |
| *(12* | *Anchovies (optional)* | *4 for each pepper half)* |

## METHOD

**PRE-HEAT** oven 160⁰C fan

**PEEL** Tomatoes (submerge for 1 min in boiling water, drain & peel)

**CUT** Tomatoes into quarters

**TRIM** Stalks of Peppers to about ¼ of an inch – do not cut the stalk away completely

**CUT** Peppers in half horizontally

**TAKING CARE** not to perforate the Pepper shell cut away the pith and shake out the seeds

**PLACE** the prepared Pepper halves cut side upwards in an ovenproof dish

**PEEL** and cut Garlic into thick lengthways segments

**SHARE** the Tomato segments between the Peppers

**TUCK** Garlic between Tomato segments

**PLACE** Anchovies (if using) across the tops of the now stuffed Peppers

**MEASURE** 3 teaspoons of Olive Oil into each Pepper

**BAKE** centre of the oven for 45 mins or until the edges of Peppers are slightly blackened

**SERVE** with Crusty Bread.

# Cheese & Asparagus (or Onion) Flan

*This is a useful recipe, as it freezes well cooked or uncooked. Simple Vegetarian meal with salad but don't hesitate to make it because you are not a vegetarian – it does taste good. Makes for two*

**INGREDIENTS**

| | | |
|---|---|---|
| 3 | Average sized Onions | Roughly chopped |
| 150 g | Cheddar Cheese | Grated |
| 50 g | Plain Flour | |
| 3 tbsp | Milk | |
| 1 tsp | Salt | |
| 1 Sheet | Short crust Pastry | |

**METHOD**
**PRE-HEAT** Oven to 220°C fan
**ROLL** out Pastry on a smooth floured surface
**LINE** 18 cm tin with Pastry
**TRIM** edges neatly and
**SET ASIDE** in a cool place
**PLACE** Asparagus (Onions) and Salt in a saucepan, barely cover with cold Water
**BOIL** for 2/3 minutes
**STRAIN** off but leave in saucepan
**ADD** Flour to Asparagus (Onions); turn to coat evenly.
**TIP** floured Asparagus (Onions) into pastry tin
**ADD** Cheese, spread over Asparagus (Onions)
**SPOON** Milk evenly over surface
**BAKE** for 15/20 minutes or until it looks golden brown

# Chicken & Broccoli Casserole

*I discovered this whilst in Australia – you will note a number of my recipes come from friends there. This makes a meal for four. You might as well make the full amount and then put half in the freezer against a future need*

## INGREDIENTS

| | | |
|---|---|---|
| 500 g | Fresh Broccoli | Trimmed into individual florets |
| 2 | Chicken Breasts | Skinned |
| 25 g | Plain Flour | |
| 30 g | Butter | |
| 300 ml | Double Cream | Use single if you prefer |
| ½ cup | Water | |
| 1 | Chicken Stock Cube | |
| Pinch | Salt, Pepper, Nutmeg | |
| ½ tsp | Dry Mustard | |
| 125 g | Cheese – Gruyere, Parmesan even Cheddar | Whichever chosen needs to be grated |

## METHOD

**STEAM** Broccoli for about 5 minutes
**DRAIN** well and arrange in shallow casserole dish
**ARRANGE** Chicken Breasts over the Broccoli
**MELT** Butter in a wide saucepan or a deep frying pan
**STIR** in the Flour stirring all the time for about 1 minute
**ADD** gradually the Water and Crumbled Stock Cube
**STIR** well
**MIX** in Cream, Nutmeg and Grated Cheese
**STIR** over a low heat till Cheese melts
**SEASON** with Salt and Pepper
**POUR** Sauce over Chicken and
**COOK** in a moderate oven160ºC fan for 30 Minutes or until Chicken is cooked

# MEALS TO ENTERTAIN

## Moussaka

*We used to have this quite a lot and it was a pleasure to find the recipe and "do it again". Got some in the freezer and I'm looking forward to a second helping.*

**INGREDIENTS**

| | | |
|---|---|---|
| 2 | Medium-sized Aubergines | Cut lengthwise into 0.5cm slices. |
| 40 g x 2 | Butter | 2 separate lots |
| 2 tbsp X 2 | Oil | 2 separate lots |
| 2 | Large Onions | Sliced |
| 450 g | Minced Lamb or Beef | |
| 150 ml | Water | |
| 2 tbsp | Tomato Puree | |
| 1 | Egg beaten | |
| 50 g | English Cheddar | Grated |
| | Salt & freshly Ground Pepper | To taste |
| | Cheese sauce | See White Sauce in Tips for this |

**METHOD**
**SPRINKLE** Aubergines with Salt and let stand for about 30/40 mins
**RINSE** and drain thoroughly
**FRY** Aubergines in large pan with one lot of Butter and Oil until golden on both sides
**REMOVE** from pan and put on one side
**FRY** Onions in second lot of Butter and Oil until pale gold
**ADD** Meat and cook till browned on all sides
**ADD** Water and Tomato Puree
**SEASON** to taste with Salt & Pepper
**LINE** base of a square or oblong ovenproof dish with half the Aubergines
**COVER** with Meat mixture
**ARRANGE** remaining Aubergines on the top
**BEAT** Egg into White Sauce
**POUR** Sauce over Aubergines
**SPRINKLE** with Cheese
**BAKE** at 180ºC fan for 45mins. You need the top to be golden then it's ready to enjoy

# Harissa Lamb with Chickpea & Orange Couscous

*This is a very easy meal to make and tastes as if you had spent ages over a hot stove on it. But do choose good lamb steaks. Serves two*

## INGREDIENTS

| 2 x 100g | Lean Lamb Steaks | |
|---|---|---|
| 200 g | Chickpeas | From a can, otherwise it's an overnight job |
| 120 ml | Hot Vegetable Stock | |
| 75 g | Couscous | |
| 4 | Spring Onions | Chopped finely |
| 1 tsp | Orange the zest of | |
| 2 tsp | Harissa Paste | |
| 1 tsp | Olive oil | |
| 1 tsp | Ground Coriander | |
| 1 tbsp | Mint | Chopped finely |

## METHOD
**PREPARE** Hot Stock
**POUR** Stock over Couscous in a large bowl
**STIR** in Orange Zest
**SET** aside for about 10 minutes allowing Couscous to swell
**HEAT** a griddle pan or the grill
**RUB** Lamb Steaks with the Harissa Paste then
**BRUSH** lightly with the Olive Oil
**COOK** for 3-4 minutes each side
**COVER** with foil and allow to rest for 2-3 minutes
**COOK** Chickpeas for 2-3 minutes then
**FLUFF UP** the Couscous
**STIR IN** the Chickpeas, Spring Onions, Coriander and Mint
**SERVE** Couscous topped with Lamb.

## Minted Lamb Tagine

*Now here's something for the pub quiz. A tagine is an earthenware dish with a conical lid and is also the name of the recipe. A Moroccan-type dish – BUT not wholly authentic - It's really a stew but is so good and easy to make. I did it when I was out all day with my lady friend and it was so good to come back to and just a large glass of wine, marvelous. A slow cooker is best or a crock-pot. The prunes are optional but do they add to the experience. Makes for 4 so some for the freezer.*

**INGREDIENTS**

| | | |
|---|---|---|
| 700 g | Stewing Lamb | Diced |
| 12 | Pearl (button) Onions | Peeled but left whole |
| 2 | Courgettes | Diced |
| 2 | Carrots | Diced |
| 1 | Green Pepper | Diced |
| 1 | Red Pepper | Diced |
| 100 g | Stoned Prunes (optional) | Halved |
| 1 | Green Chili | Seeded and Chopped |
| 1 | Large Garlic Clove | Crushed |
| 2 tbsp | Parsley | Freshly chopped |
| 2 tbsp | Mint | Freshly Chopped |
| 2 tbsp | Tomato Puree | |
| ¼ tsp | Ground Cinnamon | |
| ¼ tsp | Ground Ginger | |
| 225 g | Couscous | |
| 450 ml | Boiling Lamb stock | Or Chicken Stock |
| Pinch | Salt & Pepper | Seasoning as required |

**METHOD**

**PLACE** Lamb; the vegetables prepared as above in the Slow Cooker/Crock pot with Prunes (if using) Chili; Garlic; the Cinnamon; Ginger and Salt & Pepper

**ADD** Boiling Stock **COVER**

**COOK** on High for 3 hours or 6 on Low

**20 MINUTES** before the end of the cooking period

**PUT** Couscous in a bowl and just cover with boiling water

**PLACE** the bowl over a pan of boiling Water (or in a steamer)

**STEAM** for 15 minutes

**STIR** the Tomato Puree and one tablespoon each of Mint and Parsley into the  Tagine

**SEASON** with Salt & Pepper to taste

**SPOON** the Couscous onto the serving plates

**SPOON** the Tagine on top

**SPRINKLE** the remaining herbs before serving

# Beef Stroganoff

*A good old standby, about an hour from start to finish for good taste and something definitely moreish.*

**INGREDIENTS**

| | | |
|---|---|---|
| 300 g | Fillet Steak | Cut into 1 cm slices then 1 cm pieces |
| 50 ml | Soured Cream | |
| 200 ml | Beef Stock | |
| 25 g | Button Mushrooms | Finely Chopped |
| 1 tbsp | Butter | |
| 1 | Red Onion | Finely chopped |
| 1 tsp | Paprika | |
| 1 | Garlic clove | Finely Chopped |
| 1 tbsp | English Mustard | |
| | Olive Oil | For frying the beef |
| 3 | Sprigs of Parsley | Finely Chopped |
| | Salt & Pepper | For flavouring to taste |
| 1 | Lemon | For its juice |
| Splash | Brandy | |

**METHOD**

**SEASON** Beef with Paprika, Lemon Juice, Salt & Pepper

**SET ASIDE** for 5/6 minutes

**HEAT** the Butter in a large frying pan

**ADD** Onions and **SAUTÉ** for 2/3 minutes

**ADD** Mushrooms & Garlic

**COOK** for 5 minutes until both soft

**STIR** in the Mustard making sure that all are fully coated

**POUR** the Stock over then

**SIMMER** until liquid reduced by up to one half

**STIR IN** the Soured Cream

**SET ASIDE** for a few minutes

**PRE HEAT** Oven to 180ºC fan

**HEAT** a small amount of Olive Oil in a separate pan

**FRY** Beef turning till browned all over, about 1 minute

**STIR IN** Mushroom & Onion mixture

**ADD** Brandy

**POUR** into casserole dish

**COOK** for 15- 20 minutes until Beef fully cooked

**GARNISH** with Parsley

**SERVE** with Broccoli & Carrots to give colour.

If you want Potatoes I suggest using Sweet Potatoes

# Rosemary Chicken

*This was an old recipe, which I just revived. It is excellent. Don't forget to cook vegetables as well – I did carrots (for colour), asparagus tips, brussel sprouts and new potatoes. Remember when new potatoes are in season use them a lot as the taste they add to almost anything is distinct. This makes a meal for two*

## INGREDIENTS

| | | |
|---|---|---|
| 350 g | Chicken Breast | Cut into serving size pieces |
| 50 g<br>1 tbsp | Plain Flour | Need two separate portions |
| 40 g<br>20 g | Butter | Need two separate portions |
| 300 ml | White wine | Two 150 ml portions |
| 2 tbsp | Olive Oil | |
| 1 | Onion | Peeled and finely chopped |
| 60 ml | Water | |
| 30 ml | Crème Fraiche | |
| 1 | Chicken Stock Cube | Crumbled |
| ¼ tsp | Turmeric | |
| ½ tsp | Rosemary | Finely chopped |
| 1 | Garlic clove | Crushed |
| | Salt & Pepper to taste | |

## METHOD

**COAT** Chicken Pieces in flour

**HEAT** 1st portion of Butter and Oil in a large shallow pan

**ADD** Chicken and cook till brown on all sides

**REMOVE** Chicken from pan and put into a bowl till ready

**STIR** Onion into pan

**COOK** until tender

**ADD** I portion of Wine

**COOK** until Liquid is reduced by up to half

**REMOVE** Onions  and keep with Chicken till ready

**MELT** 2nd portion of Butter

**STIR** in 2 Tablespoons of Flour

**COOK** for 1 minute

**STIR** in Water, Stock Cube, 2nd portion Wine, Crème Fraiche, Turmeric, Rosemary and Crushed Garlic & Olive Oil

**SEASON** to taste with Salt & Pepper, **MIX** well

**STIR** until boiling **REDUCE HEAT**

**ADD** Chicken and Onions cover and simmer gently for 30 minutes until Chicken is tender.

# Chicken with Olives & Tomato Sauce

*This chicken recipe has quite a nice flavour to it although not many ingredients which helps make this easy and quick.*

## INGREDIENTS

| 4 | Chicken Thighs | Boned and skinned |
|---|---|---|
| 1 tbsp | Virgin Olive Oil | |
| 4 | Garlic Cloves | Peeled and chopped |
| 40 g | Cherry Tomatoes | |
| 2 tbsp | Capers | |
| 2 tbsp | Olives | |
| 30 g | Basil leaves | |
| Pinch | Salt & Pepper | Season to taste |

## METHOD

**PRE-HEAT** Oven to 180oC fan
**HEAT** Olive Oil in a heavy frying pan
**ADD** Garlic, Cherry Tomatoes, Capers and Olives
**SIMMER** gently for 5 minutes
**ADD** Chicken thighs and **STIR** well to ensure well combined
**TRANSFER** to a casserole dish with lid
**POSITION** on middle shelf
**COOK** 15 minutes
**REMOVE** from oven and **STIR** well to ensure Chicken well covered in the sauce
**RETURN** to the oven and cook for a further 20 minutes
**ADD** Basil leaves and leave for a few minutes before serving

# Cheddar, Bacon & Tomato Tart

*Another Waitrose (UK) recipe. This is another easy one and good. Used it a lot since I found it and I've quite a few friends for whom this is a treat. By now, if you are following me, you will realize that cooking is the very best way of expanding your social relations and as widowers we need to do this otherwise we will dry up, vegetate and be a disappointment to our departed spouses – do not go there – you are missing life!!!!!!*

## INGREDIENTS

| | | |
|---|---|---|
| 300 g | Short crust pastry | |
| 6 rashers | Smoked Streaky Bacon | Cut into 1 cm strips |
| 250 g | Cherry tomatoes | Cut in half |
| 200 g | Extra strong Mature Cheddar | Grated |
| 170 ml | Double Cream | |
| 150 ml | Semi-skimmed milk | |
| 4 medium | Eggs | Free range |
| 2 tbsp | Chopped Fresh Chives | Plus some for garnish |
| | Plain flour for dusting | |

## METHOD

**PRE-HEAT** oven to 190ºC fan
**ROLL-OUT** Pastry and ensure it will cover the bottom of a 23 cm loose-bottomed tart tin
**LINE** tin with pastry
**TRIM** edges
**PRICK** base with a fork
**LINE** tin with baking parchment and fill with Baking Beans (see below)
**BAKE** for 15 minutes or until pale golden
**REMOVE** Parchment and Beans
**COOK** at 160ºC for 5 minutes
Now **COOK** Bacon in a non-stick frying pan until crisp (4 or 5 min)
**PLACE** Tomatoes, Cheese and Bacon in tin
**BEAT** together Cream, Milk, Eggs and Chives and
**POUR** into tin
**BAKE** for 45 minutes until set and golden.
**REMOVE** Tart from tin and sprinkle the extra Chives over
**SERVE** with salad and enjoy

**This is another great one for freezing. Suggest you divide up into portion sizes; wrap in cling film and freeze – so now you have single slices for a quickie meal whenever you fancy it**

**Baking beans** are any dried beans you use to keep pastry from rising whilst it bakes prior to being filled as planned

# Chicken & Sausage Cassoulet

*Sometimes one just wants something easy, quick and tasty. So here it is. It also reminds me of my father, as he was very partial to Butter Beans. It was a frequent visitor to our plates at home.*
*Many of the ingredients can be varied i.e. different types of beans and any of a whole range of Sausages to suit your tastes*
*So, go for it – my food tester friend liked it very much.*

## INGREDIENTS

| | | |
|---|---|---|
| 4/5 | Sausages – your choice | Chipolata will suffice |
| 1 | Large Onion | Sliced |
| 400 g | Chicken Breast | In chunks if you can buy them otherwise you need them in 2 cm chunks |
| 400 g | Tinned Chopped Tomatoes | This is about 1 can |
| 400 g | Cannellini Beans | Ditto |
| 400 g | Butter Beans | Ditto |
| 15 g | Fresh Oregano | Chopped |
| 1 tbsp | Virgin Oil | For cooking |

## METHOD

**HEAT** a non-stick frying pan
**ADD** Oil and Sausages
**COOK** for about 3-4 minutes until browned on all sides
**SET** aside Sausages and
**ADD** Chicken and Onion to frying pan
**COOK** about 4-5 minutes until Chicken is browned and Onion has softened
**SLICE** Sausages into bite size pieces then
**RETURN** Sausages to the pan and
**STIR IN** both Beans and Tomatoes
**BRING TO BOIL** and then cover
**SIMMER** for 30 – 35 minutes
**STIRRING** occasionally until Chicken is thoroughly cooked and tender
**GARNISH** with Oregano and serve. Best served in large bowls and use spoons

# Chicken Schnitzel

*Now at some time or other we have had Chicken Schnitzel and will have found it lacking flavour. Now this recipe will have you and any guests really pleased at the taste. Go on try it. This makes four servings. Goes well with carrots, courgettes and broccoli*

## INGREDIENTS

| | | |
|---|---|---|
| 6 | Chicken Cutlets | Skinned and excess fat removed |
| 2 | Large Eggs | |
| 60 g | Fresh Breadcrumbs | Seeded I think is best |
| 30 g | Grated Parmesan | |
| 4 tbsp | Olive Oil | |
| 2 tbsp | Butter | |
| 1 | Garlic Clove | |
| 1 ½ tsp | Fresh Parsley | |
| 30 ml | Dry White Wine | Not an expensive one |
| 70 g | Natural Yoghurt | |
| 50 ml | Chicken Stock | |
| 3 tbsp | Fresh Lemon Juice | Keep them separate |
| 1 tbsp | Skimmed Milk | |
| Pinch | Salt & Pepper to taste | |

## METHOD

**POUND** Chicken Cutlets to reduce them to about ¼ inch in thickness –this is a critical operation as schnitzel must not be too thick

**BEAT** Eggs in a shallow bowl and

**SEPARATELY COMBINE**   Breadcrumbs and Parmesan Cheese

**ADD** Garlic, Parsley and season to taste with Salt & Pepper

**LIGHTLY DUST** the Chicken with a handful of flour

**DIP** each Cutlet first into the eggs and then the Breadcrumb Mix

**COOK**   for five minutes in a large non-stick frying pan using some of the Olive oil

**REMOVE** from pan and set aside

**COMBINE** in a small bowl the Yoghurt and Lemon Juice

**HEAT** ½ the Butter and Milk

**SEASON** well and set aside to serve later

**WIPE** the pan clean

**HEAT** remainder of Butter and **ADD** Wine Stock & Lemon Juice

**POUR** over Cutlets and

**SIMMER** for 2 mins then **SERVE**

# VEGETARIAN

## Vegetable Tagine

*Now this is a vegetarian option but it is good! This can be done in about two hours if you leave the Chick Peas out; because they need to soak overnight. Their inclusion is definitely worthwhile so suggest you work on that basis. So, to work.......*

## INGREDIENTS

| | | |
|---|---|---|
| 240 g | Couscous | |
| 100 g | Chick Peas | Soaked overnight 100 ml |
| 100 ml | Olive Oil | But have the bottle handy |
| 1 tbsp | Paprika | |
| ½ tbsp. | Ground Ginger | |
| ½ tbsp. | Dried Chilies | Crushed |
| ½ tbsp. | Ground Cumin | |
| ½ tbsp. | Ground Coriander | |
| ½ tbsp. | Ground Black Pepper | |
| 1 | Garlic Clove | Crushed with1/2 tsp salt |
| 1 | Lemon | Squeezed for juice |
| 1 | Courgette | Cut into wedges |
| 2 | Carrots | Scraped & cut into batons |
| 1 | Butternut Squash | Peeled and cut into 2cm squares |
| 2 | Parsnips | Scraped and cut into batons |
| 1 | Aubergine | Cut into wedges |
| 4 | Small Potatoes | Boiled, peeled and halved |
| 500 ml | Vegetable Stock | |
| Small | Amount of Butter | |

## METHOD

**POUR** Boiling Water over the Couscous

**ADD** a little Olive Oil and

**STIR** well

**LEAVE** to stand for 10-15 mins forking through every now and then

**PRE HEAT** Oven to 200ºC fan

**COMBINE** all the spices in a mixing bowl with Garlic, Lemon Juice and half the Olive Oil

**HEAT** the rest of the Olive Oil in a pan and cook the vegetables i.e. Carrots, Turnips, Aubergine, Parsnips & squash for about 5 – 7 minutes

**ADD** the Spice Mixture and

**STIR** to coat the vegetables

**COOK** for two more minutes

**ADD** Vegetable Stock and cook for 5 more minutes

**ADD** Courgettes, Potatoes & Chick Peas

**MIX** well then place into a casserole

**BAKE** for 25 mins or until vegetables are tender

**REMOVE** the oven and

**SPRINGLE** Rosewater on top

**DOT** Butter over the Couscous

**MICROWAVE** on medium for 5 minutes

**SERVE** all vegetables in a serving dish and the

**PILE** Couscous on top

**SERVE** with Onion Marmalade

## "Veggie" Pie

*The basis for this came from another food site renbenham.com and I thought it was good when I made it. It is. I varied it to make it a vegetarian option and it loses nothing. I took out the carrot to cook separately and give colour. Sliced mushrooms were substituted. Chick Peas replaced chicken in the original version. You will like it so will your guests*

**INGREDIENTS**

| 400 g | Chick Peas | Tinned best saves soaking overnight |
|-------|-----------|-------------------------------------|
| 25 g | Sliced Mushrooms | Again, suggest use tinned |
| 2 | Courgettes | Cubed but not too large |
| 200 g | Asparagus | Finely Chopped |
| 200 g | Crème Fraiche | |
| 1 tsp | Olive Oil | |
| 1 | Onion | Peeled & Chopped small |
| 1 | Stick Celery | Chopped |
| 315 g | Ready Rolled Puff Pastry | Need 2/3 hours for it to thaw |
| 1 tbsp | Flour | For floured surface to roll pastry out |
| 1 tbsp | Butter | To seal pastry down |
| 1 | Egg | Beaten |
| Pinch | Salt & Pepper to season | |

**METHOD**

**PRE-HEAT** oven to 180ºC fan

**HEAT** Oil in a large frying pan – the largest you've got

**ADD** Onions, Celery and fry for 5 mins – keep stirring

**ADD** Courgettes, Asparagus, Mushrooms and fry for further 3 minutes

**STIR** in Crème Fraiche and Salt & Pepper to taste

**TRANSFER** the mixture to pie dish

**UNROLL** the pastry onto a clean-floured surface

**BUTTER** the rim of the pie dish

**LIFT** the pastry over the top of the pie dish (You might need to roll the pastry out a little to ensure a fit)

**PRESS** the edges down with a fork

**TRIM** excess pastry

**BRUSH** the pastry all over with the beaten Egg

**BAKE** for 30 mins or until puffed up and golden colour

# Cheesy Spinach & other Veggies

*This is a very good "veggie" dish and you do not have to be a vegetarian to appreciate it. Spinach is one of my favourite vegetables but beware you need a large amount as it wilts dramatically when you start. But press on the taste is so good.*

**INGREDIENTS**

| 400 g | Spinach | Washed |
|-------|---------|--------|
| 1 | Large Onion | Finely chopped |
| 250 g | Courgettes | Finely chopped |
| 90 g | Butter | You need 3 X 30 g |
| 2 tbsp | Plain Flour | |
| 60 g | Cheese | Grated |
| 300 ml | Milk | |
| 1 Cup | Breadcrumbs | I prefer from seeded bead – adds interest |
| Pinch | Salt & Pepper to taste | |

**METHOD**

**PLACE** Spinach in a large saucepan and cover with water
**SIMMER** for 5 minutes
**DRAIN** and place in the bottom of your casserole dish
**HEAT** portion 1 of Butter in pan
**ADD** Onions and Courgettes
**COOK** for 2 minutes
**REMOVE** from pan to **PLACE** on top of Spinach in casserole
**MELT** portion 2 of Butter in pan
**ADD** Flour stirring until smooth
**COOK** for one minute
**GRADUALLY** add milk
**STIR** until sauce thickens
**REDUCE** heat and **ADD** Cheese, Salt & Pepper to taste
**STIR** until cheese melted
**POUR** over Onions and Courgettes
**MELT** Portion 3 of Butter
**ADD** Breadcrumbs and **COMBINE** well
**SPRINKLE** the sauce over the Onion and the Courgettes
**BAKE** in moderate oven 160ºC fan for 30 – 35 mins top should be light brown

# Cauliflower & Broccoli Cheese

*This is such a useful addition to your repertoire – it goes with almost any meat dish. Not only that I can introduce the amazing Delia Smith and her way of cooking the Cauliflower (see* **www.deliaonline.comdeliaonline-cookery-school/tech-cauliflower.html***) look for videos. There is a tremendous amount of useful stuff on her site – you may never leave it and come back to mine but if you are cooking that's great!!!*

## INGREDIENTS

| 300 g | Cauliflower or Broccoli | Half and half works well. Break into medium florets |
|---|---|---|
| 30 g | Butter | |
| 30 g | Plain Flour | |
| 250 ml | Hot Milk | |
| 2 X 30 g | Strong Cheddar Cheese | Grated. Need half for the sauce and topping |
| 2 X 15 g | Parmesan Cheese | Ditto |
| 1 tsp | Ready-made mustard | Grainy is particularly nice |
| 1 large | Pinch Cayenne Pepper | |
| 30 g | Breadcrumbs | I prefer Wholegrain seeded bread |
| | Salt | Season to your preference |

## METHOD
**UNDERCOOK** the Cauliflower and Broccoli (steam, boil or microwave or view the video)
**STRAIN** and
**REFRESH** in plenty of Cold Water and
**STRAIN** again (if not planning to eat dish immediately put to one side) otherwise
**PLACE** in Casserole dish for immediate use
**MELT** butter in pan and lift off heat
**BLEND** in Flour and "cook out" over gentle heat till grainy
**REMOVE** from heat
**STIRRING CONTINUOUSLY** gradually add the Hot Milk beating well the whole time
**BOIL** over a low heat, stirring all the while until sauce thickens
**SEASON** with Cayenne Pepper; Salt and Mustard
**STIR** through first portion of Cheddar Cheese and Parmesan
**POUR** sauce over Cauliflower and Broccoli
**COMBINE** reserved topping cheeses and Breadcrumbs
**SPRINKLE** Breadcrumb mixture evenly over top of sauce
**BROWN** under hot grill till golden 170ºC fan for about 20/25 mins

This is a good vegetable dish to accompany any roast meat dish.
It is particularly good if you are preparing a "Virgin Roast" i.e. no meat at all, and vegetables such as carrots, red cabbage roast potatoes and parsnips.

# SOMETHING SPECTACULAR or ADVENTUROUS

## Spanish Omelette (or Tortilla)

*Now here's an interesting recipe which although it takes a little preparation could be in the "Quick, Easy and Spectacular" class. Certainly, the taste is spectacular and with so few ingredients. The purists would say that this is a "Peasant Tortilla" because of the use of an onion. Don't worry about them just make it!*

**INGREDIENTS**

| 600 g | Potatoes | Peeled and sliced to about 2 x £2 coins |
|---|---|---|
| 4 | Large Eggs | |
| 1 | Onion | Thinly sliced |
| | Extra Virgin Olive Oil | |
| | Salt & Pepper | To season to taste |

**METHOD**
**PAT** Potatoes dry and put them in a bowl to season with Salt & Pepper
**HEAT** about 2 cm of Olive Oil in a large frying pan
**ADD** Potatoes to the Oil when hot and
**ADD** more Oil to make sure Potatoes are covered (you can reuse the Oil)
**COOK** for 20 mins on a low heat and if they begin to break up don't worry
**REMOVE** Potatoes after cooking with a slotted spoon into a strainer to drain off excess oil
**NOW BEAT** the Eggs in another largish bowl and season
**FRY** the Onions in a separate pan for 8-10 mins, stir often, till caramelised
**ADD** Onions to the Egg mixture
**COMBINE** the now cooled Potatoes with the Egg mixture and stir well
**Add** the combined mixture to the frying pan now drained of the Oil and over a medium heat
**COOK** for 6 mins for one side
**TAKE** a late larger than the frying pan
**PLACE** over the pan and turn the tortilla over and
**COOK** the other side for 6 mins.
**SLIDE** the Tortilla out on to a serving plate and after cooling a little **DIVE IN**.

# Salmon En Croute

 *This is delicious. Not being fond of much fish I find recipes with Salmon a godsend and there are some more to come. I have a suspicion that the basis for this recipe originally was a BBC Good Food recipe.*

## INGREDIENTS

| 3 tbsp | Olive Oil | |
|---|---|---|
| 150 g | Tin Chopped Mushrooms | |
| 2 x 350g | Skinned Salmon Fillets | |
| 5 sheets | Filo pastry | |
| 3 | Medium sized Shallots | Finely Chopped |
| 3 | Crushed Garlic Cloves | |
| ½ | Lemon for juice | *See note below* |
| 100 g | Watercress | Chopped |
| 2 tbsp | Dill | Finely chopped |
| Pinch | Salt | |
| 2 tbsp | Chive | Finely chopped |
| 2 ½ tbsp | Crème fraiche | |

## METHOD

**HEAT** 2 tablespoons of Oil in large non-stick frying pan.

**ADD** Shallots and **FRY** for 2-3 minutes to soften, now

**ADD** Mushrooms and Garlic and fry over high heat for 3-4 minutes, stirring frequently, until Shallots are golden

**POUR** in the Lemon Juice

**REMOVE** from heat

**STIR** in the Watercress and it will wilt from the warmth of the pan

**STIR** in Dill and Chives; season with a little Salt

**SET** aside to cool

**PRE-HEAT** oven to 180ºC

**LINE** a baking tray with baking parchment

**STIR** Crème Fraiche into the mushroom mix **when** it is cool.

**LAY** one sheet of Filo Pastry on the work surface after lightly dusting with flour

**BRUSH** some of the remaining oil all over the Filo Pastry, then

**LAY** another sheet of on top of the first and again brush with oil, and then follow through with two more sheets

**LAY** one of the Salmon Fillets skin-side up across the width of the filo about 1/3rd along.

**SEASON** with Pepper

**SPOON & SPREAD** the cooled Mushroom mixture over the top of the fillet

**LAY** the second fillet on top

**SEASON** again

**FOLD** the short end of the Pastry nearest the Salmon over the Salmon then
**BRING** the other end right over to cover the Salmon completely so the join can be underneath.
**FOLD** pastry ends as neatly as you can
**BRUSH** the outside with remainder of Oil.
*To this point can be prepared up to 4 hours before needed but do chill it.*
**TRANSFE**R the Salmon parcel onto the baking sheet
Bake for 25 minutes
**CHECK** Progress and if browning too quickly place a piece of foil loosely over.
**REMOVE** from oven and let it rest for 3 minutes or so before slicing and serving

**Serve with carrots, asparagus tips and new potatoes**

*Note:* **Lemon Juice – I just buy it as it saves buying lemons and is easier to have at hand – you frequently need lemon juice**

# Chicken à la King – Anne's recipe

*Now this could be your first entertaining dish – it was mine!*
*There is a note in Techniques Section dealing with poaching the Chicken but buying a BBQ Chicken works almost as well. Carrots and Broccoli go well with this and provide a splash of colour.*
*Makes 4 servings*

## INGREDIENTS

| 500 g | Cooked, diced, chicken breast Use BBQ for speed | Poached is nicer if there is time (See below) |
|---|---|---|
| 40 g | Small white mushrooms, peeled & sliced | Could use tinned |
| 2 | Medium Onions | Finely chopped |
| 1 | Green pepper | ditto |
| 1 | Red pepper | ditto |
| 2 x 30g | Portions of Butter | You will need to use half of this at a time so easier to weigh amount in two dishes. |
| 50 g | Plain flour | |
| ¾ tsp. | Salt | This is personal taste |
| ½ tsp. | Paprika | This is personal taste |
| 250 ml | Milk – it really does not matter. Suit yourself – full cream or skinny | |
| 250 ml | Chicken Stock | |
| 2 tbsp | Ground Parmesan cheese | Really only to give it colour when finished |
| | Parsley for garnish | |

## METHOD

**FRY** Peppers for 4 – 5 mins in half the Butter – keep stirring as they brown all of a sudden – *they really do.*
**REMOVE** from pan, drain on plate lined with kitchen paper
**WIPE** out pan with kitchen paper.
***To make the sauce (otherwise known as "roux")***
**HEAT** Milk and Stock separately then combine
**MELT** remaining Butter in cleaned out pan, lift off heat and
**BLEND** in Flour and "cook out" the sauce over gentle heat till grainy – keep stirring – this happens quickly so watch out
**REMOVE** from heat.

**STIR** in gradually the hot Milk and Stock, continuously stirring
**RETURN** to low heat
**BRING** to boil over low heat, stirring all the time, until sauce thickens, can take time.  No, it **will** take time. I have done it at home and in some else's kitchen and it was a far longer period. Be patient you will get a reward
**ADD** Salt & Paprika and taste to check seasoning
**ADD** cooked Chicken (by whatever means you have used), Peppers and Mushroom and Onions.
**MIX** together so all constituents are coated with the sauce.
**PLACE** into dish for cooking
**SPREAD** Parmesan cheese over and straight into the oven.
**PRE HEAT** oven to 170$^0$C fan
**COOK** for 25 minutes and until golden on top.

## Options re Chicken Meat

1       Pre-cooked BBQ chicken from supermarket

2       A 350 g raw Chicken breast poached yields approx. 260 g
        cooked meat.

## Poached Chicken

**PLACE** Chicken Breasts in a single layer in a saucepan
**ADD** for each Breast ½ roughly chopped Onion; ½ Bay leaf; 1/2 tsp Stock cube
**COVER** with cold water
**BRING** to boil
**LOWER** heat and simmer for 8 – 12 minutes
**CHECK** Chicken fully cooked (insert skewer – juices should run clear, if even slightly pink continue cooking for a further few minutes)
**REMOVE** from heat and cool quickly – if possible still in poaching water; this can be used to make the stock, which will be needed for this recipe.

# Asparagus Quiche, Chicken Croquettes & Mint Salad

*This is a combination of three, which come together as a great meal. It is good because you can make the Croquettes the day before needed – the quiche earlier in the day and salad last - less pressure on the day. Again, thanks to Beth in Australia for this one. I suspect she makes it better than me. Makes enough for two.*

## INGREDIENTS – Chicken Croquettes

| 250 g | Chicken | Chopped. Could buy BBQ chicken from supermarket and chop small |
|---|---|---|
| 200 g | Back Bacon | Chopped small |
| 60 g | Butter | |
| 1 | Medium Onion | Finely chopped |
| 2 tsp | Curry Powder | |
| 45 g | Plain Flour | |
| 1 cup & ½ cup | Milk | Measure separately as are required at differing stages |
| 65 g | Seasoning of choice | I prefer Sage & Onion |
| 65 g | Cheese – your choice | Grated |
| 2 | Eggs | Lightly beaten |
| 2 tbsp | Olive Oil | |
| 150 g | Dried Breadcrumbs | |

## METHOD
**MELT** Butter in pan
**ADD** Onion, Bacon, Curry Powder
**COOK** stirring for a few moments, don't let Onions brown
**STIR** in Flour cook for a further minute
**GRADUALLY** Stir in Milk and keep stirring over heat until mixture boils and thickens.
**REMOVE** from heat and stir in Chicken, seasoning and Cheese
**SPREAD** onto tray covered with plastic wrap and refrigerate until cold
**SHAPE** mixture into Croquettes
**COMBINE** Eggs and Milk to combine
**COAT** Croquettes in Egg and Milk mixture then
**COAT** Croquettes in Breadcrumbs
**COOK** lightly in frying pan with Virgin Oil

The Croquettes can be cooked and refrigerated for up to 12 hours before being required. If left overnight **COOK** on a baking tray uncovered for about 15 mins on 160ºC fan.

Now having safely made the Croquettes turn to the Quiche

## INGREDIENTS Quiche

| 15 g | Butter | |
|------|--------|---|
| 1 | Onion | Finely chopped |
| 1 | Clove Garlic | Crushed |
| 2 | Eggs | |
| 150 g | Sour Cream | |
| 70 g | Tasty Cheese – your choice | Grated |
| 15 g | Parmesan Cheese | Grated |
| 1 tbsp | Self-raising Flour | |
| 1/3 cup | Milk | |
| 1 Can | Asparagus Spears | |
| 150 g | Breadcrumbs | |
| Touch | Paprika | |

## METHOD

**HEAT** Butter in pan; add Onion and cook stirring until Onions soft

**STIR** in Garlic and Breadcrumbs

**PRESS** mixture evenly over base of 23 cm (9 inch) quiche dish

**SEPARATELY** blend together Eggs, Sour Cream, Cheeses, Flour and Milk until smooth

**POUR** slowly into quiche dish.

**TOP** with Asparagus sprinkled lightly with Paprika

**BAKE** 35 mins at 160°C fan or until set.

Now on to the Salad

## INGREDIENTS - Minted Tomato & Pea Salad

| 250 g | Peas | Fresh or frozen |
|-------|------|---|
| ½ | Cucumber | |
| 2 | Shallots | Chopped |
| 125 g | Cherry Tomatoes | Quartered |
| ½ cup | Virgin Oil | |
| 1 tbsp | Chopped Mint | |
| 1 Clove | Garlic | Crushed |

## METHOD

**BOIL, STEAM** or **MICROWAVE** Peas until tender

**DRAIN** and **RINSE** under cold water

**CUT** Cucumber in half lengthwise and remove seeds

**SLICE** Cucumber thinly also lengthwise – say 5 cm (2 inches)

**MIX** Oil, White Vinegar, Chopped Mint and Garlic together to make dressing

**COMBINE** Peas, Cucumber, Shallots and Tomatoes in bowl

**ADD dressing** – ensure well combined and it's ready to serve

**NOW** you are ready to heat the Croquettes and then serve with a portion of the Quiche and a serving of Salad.

## Salmon & Dill Tian

*Anne developed this from the Hairy Bikers programme on BBC. I've made also some amendments having successfully brought this all together to the approval of guests. By the time you read this friends from America will be, hopefully, amazed at what a widower can do!!!*
*It's a four-parter and I think they are special as you can take time 24 hours from start to finish and deliver a meal with little apparent fuss.*
*Makes an awesome romantic dinner for two*

### PART 1 POTATO GALETTES
### INGREDIENTS

| 300 g | Potatoes | Need to have a diameter of about 5 cm. |
|-------|----------|----------------------------------------|
| 50 g | Butter | |
| Pinch | Salt & Pepper | Freshly ground |
| Sheet | Baking Parchment | |

### METHOD
**PRE-HEAT** Oven 160ºC fan

**PEEL** Potatoes then

**SLICE** thinly, no thicker than a £1 coin. A Mandolin is best for this but not every kitchen will have one

**CUT** two 12 cm circles from the Baking Parchment.

**PLACE** Potatoes in a large bowl

**MELT** the Butter either in a saucepan over low heat or in the microwave

**POUR** the melted Butter over the Potato slices, mix well to coat

**SEASON** to taste with Salt and Fresh Ground Pepper

**PLACE** the parchment discs on a baking tray then

**ARRANGE** the Potato slices, overlapping, in concentric circles on the discs

**BAKE** for 25/30 minutes or until the slices are beginning to brown

**SET ASIDE** to cool

**COVER** with Clingfilm and chill in the fridge till needed. ***I usually do this the day before needed.*** Now let's move on to the **SALMON AND DILL TIAN,** which can also be put in the fridge overnight

## PART 2 SALMON & DILL TIAN
### INGREDIENTS

| | | |
|---|---|---|
| 4 tbsp | Crème fraiche | |
| 1 | Spring Onion | Trimmed and finely sliced |
| 1 tbsp | Baby capers | Alternatively, finely chopped green olives |
| ½ | Small Lemon | The other half you will need for the salad |
| 1 tbsp | Fresh Dill | Finely chopped |
| 150 g | Hot-smoked Salmon | Not found in every Supermarket |
| | Sunflower oil | For Greasing |
| | Salt and black Pepper | Freshly ground |

### METHOD
**MIX** Crème Fraiche, Spring Onion, Capers (green olives), Lemon Juice and Dill in a bowl until well combined.

**SEASON** to taste with Salt and Pepper

**FLAKE** the hot-smoked Salmon into pieces discarding the skin

**FOLD** the Salmon into the Crème Fraiche mixture

**GREASE** two 9 cm Chef's Rings with a little oil

**LINE** with cling film

**SPOON** half of the mixture into each, smoothing and compressing down with the back of a spoon.

**PLACE** on a Baking tray and cover with Clingfilm

**CHILL** in the fridge for at least one hour – but best overnight

Remember to take them out well before you need them, especially if they have been in the fridge overnight. Next the dill and mustard dressing. You need a jar with a screw top for this

## PART 3 DILL & MUSTARD DRESSING
### INGREDIENTS

| | | |
|---|---|---|
| 1 | Medium egg yolk | |
| ½ tsp | Caster sugar | |
| 2 tbsp | Sunflower oil | |
| 2 tbsp | White wine vinegar | |
| 1 tsp | Dijon Mustard | |
| 1 tbsp | Dill | Finely chopped |

### METHOD
**PLACE** Egg Yolk, Vinegar, Mustard, Sugar, and Oil in the jar. Screw top on firmly

**SHAKE** hard

**STIR** in Dill

**SEASON** to taste with Salt and/or Black Pepper
That's it. Into fridge till required.

Finally, to be prepared fresh at the last moment – the Salad
## PART 4 FENNEL & APPLE SALAD
### INGREDIENTS

| ½ | Small Fennel | Trimmed and finely sliced. Put into bowl with water but adding the lemon juice you saved earlier |
|---|---|---|
| ½ | Red-Skinned Apple | Cored and thinly sliced |
| 2-3 tbsp | Fresh Flat-Leafed Parsley | Chopped |
| 2 tsps | Lemon Juice | Freshly Squeezed |

### METHOD
**DRAIN** the Fennel well
**PLACE** into a bowl with the Apple slices, Chopped Parsley and Lemon Juice
**SEASON** to taste as before
**MIX** until well combined
### TO SERVE

**PLACE** a Galette into the centre of each serving plates
**CAREFULLY** removing the Clingfilm from the Tian.
**TURN** onto the Galette and remove the Clingfilm altogether
**PLACE** a little of the salad to the side of the Galette and
**SPOON** the dill and mustard dressing over the salad
**Enjoy!!!**

# PART TWO SWEETS, PUDS, ETC.

**TRADITIONAL PUDDINGS** Mostly these remind us of our childhood and the recipes our mothers frequently made. I thought it would be good to give them a fresh airing and I bet they will be very well received by a younger generation.

**QUICK**     This section is mainly about fruit. Use whatever fruit is in season. Almost any of these recipes can be used with alternative fruit – except Gooseberry Fool. Now that is one to watch – there were only 4 punnets of Gooseberries in my local store this year. So just be ready when you see a new season fruit.

**EASY & SOME SPECTACULAR**     The first few are easy and so are the others but you need time – overnight in some cases in order to deliver the 'Spectacular' with which you would like to delight your guests. Grown up children find it difficult to recognise with what insouciance you can produce for example a flaming Crepe Suzette. Have Fun.

**CAKES (just in case)**     I am not much into cakes really but the following do stand me in good stead. There are frequent times when for some charity event a couple of Fruit Loaf Cakes are ideal to add to the choices on offer with tea. And Dundee Cakes are great for raffling at such events. Biscuits are good to have around and look better than bought packets and, of course, Scones go down well for a Summer teatime.

# TRADITIONAL

## Traditional English Bread & Butter Pudding

 *I've found this recipe causes a stir when served - I guess because it is old-fashioned but very acceptable all the same. If you serve this with another oven cooked meal both can usually be done at the same time leaving you, the host, more time to chat/socialise with your guests.*

**INGREDIENTS**

| 55 g | Soft Butter | To spread on bread |
|---|---|---|
| 10 slices | White Bread | Cut either diagonally or in rectangles whichever fits the dish best |
| 50 g | Raisins and Sultanas | Roughly 50/50 |
| ¼ tsp | Nutmeg | Freshly ground is best |
| ¼ tsp | Cinnamon | |
| 350 ml | Milk | Full cream is best – forget waist |
| 50 ml | Double Cream | |
| 2 large | Free range Eggs | |
| 25 g | Sugar | In 2 portions 15 g and 10 g |
| 1 tsp | Vanilla Extract | |

**METHOD**

**GREASE** 1 litre pie dish with a little of the Butter

**SPREAD** each slice of Bread with remaining Butter

**COVER** the base of the dish with overlapping slices of Bread, Butter side up

**SPRINKLE** half Raisins/Sultanas over Bread; then lightly with a little Nutmeg & Cinnamon

**REPEAT** with another layer(s) till dish filled.

**MIX** Milk and cream then

**HEAT**S gently **do not boil.**

**BEAT** in a large bowl the Eggs with the 15 g portion Sugar and Vanilla extract till light and airy – pale in colour.

**POUR** warm Milk/Cream over Eggs beating all the time

**POUR** the Egg mixture slowly and evenly over the Bread

**GENTLY** press the surface with your hand to push the Bread into the liquid

**SPRINKLE** the remaining 10g Sugar over the surface and leave to one side for 30 mins

**BAKE** at 180⁰C fan until surface is golden brown and the pudding well risen - about 40/45 minutes cooking usually

**SERVE** hot with Double Cream or Custard.

## Bread Pudding

*Now here is a family favourite – two generations; my mother made it for her children and my wife made it for our children. It's an easy one and you can bet it will go down well with the grandchildren!!!!*

**INGREDIENTS**

| 250 g | White Bread | Approx. 6 – 8 slices |
|---|---|---|
| 90 g | Brown Sugar | |
| 60 g | Butter | It used to be margarine for my mother |
| 120 g | Mixed fruit | |
| ½ tsp | Mixed spice | Or freshly ground Nutmeg |
| 1 | Egg | Lightly beaten |
| 250 ml | Milk | |

**METHOD**
**PLACE** Bread in a large mixing bowl
**POUR** Water over Bread then squeeze it out (a sieve helps here)
**ADD** Dried Fruit, Sugar, Egg and Mixed Spice (nutmeg)
**MIX** Well
**MELT** Butter whilst heating the Milk
**STIR** into the Bread Mixture
**TIP** into lightly buttered casserole dish – square is best
**PRE HEAT** Oven to 160ºC fan
**BAKE** 1½ hours
**SPRINKLE** with a little Granulated Sugar when removed from oven
**ALLOW** to cool in the dish

Can be served with Custard, in slices (which we took to school), or ice cream

# Queen of Puddings

*This has been a family favourite for a long while. I have just very satisfactorily revisited the recipe and it is still a favourite*

**INGREDIENTS**

| 1 pint | Milk | |
|--------|------|---|
| 110 g | Fresh white Breadcrumbs | |
| 10 g | Butter | |
| 25 g X 2 | Caster Sugar | |
| 3 | Eggs | May need another to get enough white |
| 3 tbsp | Raspberry Jam | |
| 1 | Lemon | For Grated Rind |

**METHOD**
**PRE-HEAT** oven to 180ºC fan
**BOIL** the milk
**REMOVE** from heat and **STIR** in the Butter, Breadcrumbs, half the Sugar and the Lemon Rind
**LEAVE** for 20 minutes for Breadcrumbs to swell
**SEPARATE** the Eggs and beat the Yolks: ADD to the Breadcrumb mixture
**BUTTER** the pie dish generously
**POUR** mixture into the pie dish and spread out evenly
**BAKE** in centre of oven for 30 – 35 minutes or until set
**MEANWHILE** melt the Jam over a low heat; when pudding ready
**REMOVE** from the oven and spread the Jam evenly over mixture
**BEAT** the Egg Whites until stiff then
**WHISK** in the balance of the Sugar and
**SPOON** this Meringue over the pudding
**SPRINKLE** a teaspoon of Caster Sugar over it all
**BAKE** for a further 10 – 15 minutes until golden brown

# Eve's Pudding

*This is an easy Apple Pudding, as you might imagine from the name. Just what the doctor ordered*

## INGREDIENTS

| | | |
|---|---|---|
| 450 g | Cooking Apples (or Pink Lady in Australia) | Peeled, cored and sliced |
| 75 g & 100 g | Caster sugar | For Apples & For Sponge Mixture |
| 100 g | Self-Raising Flour | |
| 100 g | Butter | |
| 2 | Eggs | Beaten |
| 2 tsp | Fresh Milk | |
| Pinch | Salt | |

## METHOD

**PRE-HEAT** Oven to 180°C fan

**SIFT** Flour and Salt into bowl

**CREAM** Butter and Sugar until fluffy

**ADD** Beaten Eggs a little at a time with a spoonful of Flour, beat well after each addition

**FOLD** in remaining Flour alternatively with remaining Milk

**GREASE** an ovenproof dish of about 1.4 litres

**ARRANGE** Apple in layers in dish sprinkling Sugar between the layers

**POUR** the Sponge mixture over Apples

**BAKE** for 1-hour check after 50 mins and insert a skewer. If it comes out clean the pudding is done – if not leave for the hour and check again.

**This can be served with fresh double cream or, my favourite, custard**

**You can use Rhubarb, Gooseberries or Apples with Blackberries added.**

# Pineapple Upside-down Pudding

*This has been a family favourite for many a year especially with the children but they, having left the nest a long time ago, I had forgotten about it until I found it in Anne's recipe collection. I made it recently and it worked well – will do it again for Grandchildren.*

**INGREDIENTS**

| | | |
|---|---|---|
| 60 g | Butter | |
| 110 g | Light Brown Sugar | |
| 4 slices | Pineapple | Tinned but drained |
| 75 g | Self-Raising Flour | |
| 100 g | Caster Sugar | |
| 2 | Eggs | |
| 6 | Glace Cherries | |
| 1 tsp | Baking Powder | |
| 1 tsp | Vanilla Extract | |
| ¼ tsp | Salt | |
| 1 tbsp | Butter | To be melted at the last moment |

**METHOD**
**PRE-HEAT** the oven to 160°C fan
**DRAIN** Pineapple of juice to avoid making the mixture damp
**USE** a heavy ovenproof frying pan – I used an Omelette pan
**MELT** Butter over a low heat.
**REMOVE** from heat and
**SPRINKLE** the Brown Sugar evenly over the pan
**ARRANGE** the Pineapple pieces over the bottom of the pan
**PLACE** Cherries around the Pineapple.
**LEAVE** whilst the next stage is dealt with
**NEED** 3 bowls a larger one and 2 smaller ones
**MIX** Flour, Baking Powder and Salt in a small bowl
**SEPARATE** the Eggs – the Whites into the large bowl
**PLACE** Yolks in remaining bowl
**WHISK** Egg Whites until you can form soft peaks – this takes longer than you imagine but necessary
**ADD** Caster Sugar gradually constantly beating until stiff
**BEAT** Egg Yolks at high speed until thick and yellow
**MIX** the Egg Yolks and the Flour mixture together with a Spatula
**NOW MIX** into the Egg Whites until all blended
**ADD** the tablespoon of melted Butter and the Vanilla Extract
**SPREAD** evenly over the Pineapple in the pan
**BAKE** for 30 – 35 minutes

**LOOSEN** the edges of the pudding with a knife
**COOL** for about 5 minutes then
**TURN** out on the serving plate.
**SERVE** and be surprised. Custard goes well with this

## Bannoffi Pie

*This was always a family favourite and is so simple but you must plan for the Condensed Milk you need does have to be "boiled" the day before and cooled down.*

**INGREDIENTS**

| 150 g | Digestive Biscuits | |
|---|---|---|
| 75 g | Butter | |
| 2 Cans | Condensed Milk | |
| 3 or 4 | Bananas depends on size | |
| 250 ml | Double Cream | |
| | Chilled bar of Chocolate | Or Chocolate Flake |

**METHOD**
**PLACE** Unopened Tins of Condensed Milk in a largish saucepan and cover with water
**BRING** the water to a boil and hold at the boil for about 2 hours – topping up water as necessary
**TOTALLY** cool – best-done overnight
**PLACE** the Biscuits in a plastic bag and crush them with a rolling pin – leave no large lumps
**MELT** Butter
**COMBINE** Butter and Biscuits
**PRESS** the Crumb mixture into the base and sides of a flan tin.
**WHIP** the Double Cream to a very stiff state then put in fridge
**OPEN** the Tins of Condensed Milk
**SPOON** onto the Biscuit mixture and smooth the top (it will be quite stiff)
**SLICE** sufficient Bananas to cover the top
**SPREAD** the Whipped cream over the Bananas – ensure all Bananas are covered to save them going brown
**GRATE** Chilled Chocolate Bar (or use Chocolate Flake crushed)
**SPRINKLE** over the Cream and there you are

**Note: it is best not to assemble pie more than two/three hours before eating – it can rest in the fridge. If there is any left over it can be eaten the next day even if there is some browning of the bananas – will still be delicious**

# Apple (and almost any other fruit) Crumble

*This is great because you can make the crumble mixture and freeze until you have the fruit you want. What I do when fruit is in a glut is prepare the fruit, apples say, and freeze portions till needed then you have the topping ready. That way preparation and assembly is easy - bingo!*

## INGREDIENTS

| | | |
|---|---|---|
| 150 g | Plain flour | |
| 100 g | Hard butter | |
| 50 g | Sugar | |
| 1 kg | Cooking apples (or whichever fruit you have) | Bramleys are best in UK. In Australia Pink Lady |
| 2 tbsp | Water | |

## METHOD
### Crumble Topping
**PLACE** Flour and Butter into mixing bowl
**CUT** butter through Flour, then rub-in till it resembles fine Breadcrumbs. See Techniques/tips
**STIR** in sugar

### Fruit Filling
**PEEL CORE & SLICE** Apples (or whichever fruit)
**PLACE** in dish with water,
**COVER** and microwave till soft 3- 4 minutes.
**SWEETEN** to taste when cooked
**TIP** onto dish to cool

**SPRINKLE** Crumble topping over fruit
**BAKE** 180°C fan for 25 – 30 minutes until looks and smells good.

**This works for any fruit even tinned fruit.**

# Pancakes

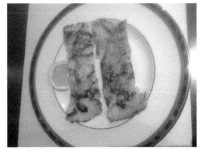

*Pancakes are a useful standby so let's learn how. Preparation time only 5 mins. This is also the base for Yorkshire puddings, Crepe Suzettes, Fritters etc. We always loved these rolled up with fresh lemon or orange juice and sugar*

**INGREDIENTS**

| 100 g | Plain Flour | |
|---|---|---|
| 1 | Egg | |
| 150 ml X 2 | Fresh Milk | |
| Pinch | Salt | |
| 15 g | Melted Butter | Or Oil for frying |
| *(40 g* | *Melted Butter* | *If making Yorkshire Pudding)* |

**METHOD**

**MIX** Flour and Salt in a bowl
**PUT** Butter in microwave to melt – 10 to15 secs should do
**BREAK** the Egg into bowl
**ADD** slowly one portion of Milk
**BEATING** all the time to create a smooth batter
**POUR** in remaining Milk
**STIR** in 2/3rds melted Butter until really smooth
**BRUSH** some of remaining Melted Butter over the base of frying pan – you will need more Melted Butter for each pancake
**PUT** over a medium heat say 160°C
**WHEN** pan and Butter are hot **POUR** in 3 tbsp of batter; tilt to ensure batter covers the base
**COOK** until Pancake moves freely
**TURN** over
**COOK** until golden
**REPEAT** until you have enough Pancakes.

**KEEP** Pancakes warm by standing them on a large plate on top of one another and the plate over a saucepan of simmering water. **ALTERNATIVELY,** you can stack them with greaseproof paper between each until you are ready to use. They will last for 2 days in an airtight tin.

**When I'm making Crepe Suzettes I always make the pancakes early and have them ready to cook for the final time so guests don't have to wait long for their treat!!**

# QUICK

## Fruit Pie

*Now this is one of my favourites. Just as soon as Redcurrants came into the shops Anne would always have Redcurrant Pie on the table and it is (in my opinion) just exquisite. But there are all sorts of other fruits, which can be used. The last one I made was with cherries and that takes some beating. I'm not going to tell you how to make pastry – just buy it. If a famous Cook like Delia Smith can write a book on "How to cheat at cooking" I feel no shame buying in what is already available.*

**INGREDIENTS**

| 400 g | Short Crust Pastry | Buy in rolls in England |
|-------|--------------------|-------------------------|
| 1 | Egg White | |
| 500 g | Fruit you plan to use | If cherries need to pit them |
| 110 g | Caster Sugar | |
| 2 tbsp | Cornflower | |
| 2 tsp | Orange Zest | |
| 150 ml | Double or Whipping Cream | |
| Few | Drops Vanilla Essence | |
| | Flour | For rolling out |

**METHOD**
**ROLL** out half the Pastry on a lightly Floured surface to a circle at least 1.5 cm wider than the size of the pie plate. Suggest a 22 cm dish, which is easily obtainable
**EASE** the Pastry into the pie plate and trim the edges.
**LIGHTLY** beat the Egg White with 1 tbsp of water and
**BRUSH** a little over the Pastry and now
**CHILL** in fridge
**PRE HEAT** the oven to 200ºC fan
**STIR** the Sugar, Cream and Corn Flour together with half Orange Zest
**ADD** Fruit and
**PILE** mixture onto the chilled pastry in pie plate
**ROLL** out the remainder of the Pastry to a circle large enough to cover the pie
**SPRINKLE** with a little more Sugar
**PLACE** the lid on top,
**SEAL** the edges and
**TRIM** the excess
**GLAZE** with remainder of Egg White
**BAKE** in the upper part of the oven for approx. 30minutes until golden and crisp
**SERVE** with Cream flavoured with remainder of Zest and Vanilla.

# Apricot Brandy & Pecan Waffles

## INGREDIENTS

| | | |
|---|---|---|
| 6 | Ripe Apricots buy 2 days in advance as they are rarely re enough in the store | Stoned & quartered |
| 2 | Ready-made Waffles | Buy in from store |
| 25 g | Pecan halves | |
| 4 tbsp | Maple Syrup | |
| 2 tbsp | Apricot Brandy | |
| 1 | Lemon | Juice needed |
| | Ice Cream | To serve |

## METHOD

**PLACE** Apricots in a non-stick frying pan

**COOK** gently for 4 minutes, frequently turning until fruit begins to brown

**MEANWHILE** prepare Waffles per the instructions on the pack

**ADD** Pecan Halves to the fruit then

**ADD** Maple Syrup, Apricot Brandy & Lemon Juice

**BOIL** then

**SIMMER** for 1 minute

**SERVE** fruit spooned over the waffles

## Sticky Rum Bananas

### INGREDIENTS

| 25 g | Butter | |
|------|--------|---|
| 75 g | Light Muscavado Sugar | |
| 1 | Lime | Grated rind and Juice |
| 1 tsp | Vanilla Essence | |
| 3 tbsp | Rum | White or Dark |
| 200 ml | Boiling Water | |
| 3 or 4 | Bananas | Peeled and halved lengthways |

### METHOD

**USE** a slow cooker for this one
**WARM** Slow Cooker
**ADD** Butter, Sugar and Lime Rind and Juice and
**STIR** until Butter is melted
**ADD** Vanilla Extract along with Rum and Boiling Water
**PLACE** Bananas in the cooker and press them in a layer below the liquid
**COVER**
**COOK** on low for 1½ - 2 hours until Bananas are hot
**SERVE** with Vanilla Ice Cream

## Avocado Mousse

 *This is about the quickest sweet to make and is very tasteful.*

**INGREDIENTS**

| 200 g | Strawberries | Very thinly sliced |
|---|---|---|
| 3 | Ripe Avocados | May need to buy these a few days before needed to ensure ripeness |
| 50 g | Cocoa Powder | |
| 50 ml | Water | |
| 100 ml | Maple Syrup | |
| | Seeds from a vanilla pod | |

**METHOD**

**PLACE** all the ingredients, except Strawberries, together in a blender until smooth

**SCRAPING** down the sides a few times during blending

**SPOON** into dessert bowls

**TOP** with the sliced Strawberries.

## Peach Melba

*A simple quick and easy sweet dish to make. Do buy the peaches a few days before you need them so they can ripen.*
*This is enough for 2 people*

**INGREDIENTS**

| 2 | Ripe Peaches | Halved and stones removed |
|---|---|---|
| 50 g | Sugar | |
| 1 | Vanilla Pod | |
| 150 g | Raspberries | |
| 2 tbsp | Icing Sugar | |
| ½ | Lemon for juice | Or use juice already bought |
| Enough | Vanilla Ice Cream | |

**METHOD**
**POACH** the Peaches covered with water and the Vanilla Pod with the Sugar for about 5 minutes until tender
**PUREE** the Raspberries, Icing Sugar and Lemon Juice in food processor
**SERVE** 2 halves of Peach per person with enough Ice Cream
**POUR** the pureed Raspberries over ice cream

**See quite easy but critical to get ripe Peaches and poach till tender**

# Gooseberry Fool

*This is a traditional English sweet around July time when gooseberries are in the shops but the season is not long so get on with it as soon as you see them. I make individual servings in tumblers and decorate with Green Seedless Grapes –Gooseberries uncooked are not the greatest taste. The icing sugar is for the grapes to be rolled in to look special.*

## INGREDIENTS

| | | |
|---|---|---|
| 450 g | Gooseberries | |
| 150 ml | Elderflower Cordial | |
| 2 | Egg Yolks | Beaten |
| 1 tsp | Arrowroot | |
| 150 ml | Milk | |
| 30 g | Sugar | |
| 150 ml | Double Cream | |
| 2 | Grapes times the number of tumblers to be filled | |
| 1 tbsp | Icing Sugar | |

## METHOD

**TOP & TAIL** the Gooseberries
**PLACE** them in a pan and together with the Cordial
**BRING** to the boil then
**SIMMER** slowly for about 5-6 minutes till soft and pulpy
**SET ASIDE** to cool in a bowl
**STRAIN** off surplus Juice but keep
**HEAT** Milk up to boiling
**BEAT** the Egg Yolks, Sugar and Arrowroot together in a jug to form Custard
**POUR** the Hot Milk into the jug
**MIX** well
**RETURN** to the pan
**HEAT** gently until the mixture thickens - careful not to boil
**EMPTY** into a clean bowl and cool
**WHIP** the Cream till it is about the same consistency as the gooseberries
**NOW** stir the Cream into the Gooseberries then
**STIR** in the Custard.
**FILL** the tumblers
**COAT** the Grapes in the juice you saved and
**ROLL** the Grapes in the Icing Sugar and put 2 on top of each tumbler
**CHILL** in fridge till ready to thrill your guests with this now somewhat unusual sweet

# Poached Apricots

*Now here is a simple dessert dish for the Summer. You do need to buy really ripe apricots – not ones to ripen at home because they don't in time.*

**INGREDIENTS**

| I bottle | Good fruity Rose wine | |
|----------|----------------------|---|
| 75 g | Golden Caster Sugar | |
| I | Vanilla Pod | Split lengthwise; cut in 4; leave seeds inside |
| 8 – 12 | Ripe Apricots | Halve and stone them before poaching |
| | Vanilla Ice-cream | Good quality |

**METHOD**

**POUR** Wine into a saucepan

**ADD** Sugar and Vanilla Pod

**STIR** over a low heat till the Sugar has completely dissolved, this happens quite quickly

**ADD** Apricots and

**COVER** and **POACH** until just softened (10 mins for halves and about 15 mins for whole Apricots)

**REMOVE** Apricots and put them aside in the bowl in which they are to be served

**BOIL** the remaining liquid hard for about 8 minutes so it becomes a thin syrup

**POUR** over the Apricots and leave to cool

**SERVE** with a good quality Vanilla Ice-cream and a piece of Vanilla Pod for decoration. A Sprig of Mint would do just as well

## Poached Pears

*Now here is a sweet that always looks amazing but is easy to make. On the other hand, you need to be on hand as it develops so pair it with a Main, which does not need so much attention!*
*Only do remember to buy the pears a couple of days in advance and leave on the worktop so that they ripen before you begin cooking*

**INGREDIENTS**

| 2 | Ripe Pears | Really ripe!! |
|---|---|---|
| 150 ml | Red Wine | Shiraz preferably |
| 2 | Oranges | Rind & Juices both needed |
| 100 g | Caster Sugar | |
| 1 | Cinnamon Stick | |
| 50 ml | Ruby Port | |
| 100 ml | Double Cream | |
| 200 ml | Boiling Water | |
| 1 | Star Anise | |
| ½ tsp | Ground Cinnamon | |

**METHOD**
**PEEL** the Pears leaving the stalks intact
**POUR** the Red Wine and Boiling Water into a medium saucepan
**ADD** Star Anise, Cinnamon, Orange Rind and Juice together with Caster Sugar
**HEAT GENTLY** until Sugar dissolved need to stir occasionally
**ADD** Pears to the pan
**CRUMPLE** a piece of greaseproof paper and run it under cold water
**COVER** the Pears in the pan
**ENSURE** Pears are under the surface of the liquid
**PLACE** lid on pan and
**SIMMER** for 25 minutes
**TRANSFER** Pears to serving bowl
**BRING** the Red Wine mixture to the boil and add the Port
**STRAIN** and pour over the Pears
**LIGHTLY** whip Cinnamon and Double Cream and
**SERVE**

# Baked Apples

*Easy and tasteful. Not too much work goes into this recipe but works very well.*

## INGREDIENTS

| | | |
|---|---|---|
| 1 | Eating Apple per person | |
| 50 g | Brown Sugar | Doesn't matter if dark or light |
| 50 g | Butter | |
| 250 g | Double Cream | |
| 1 | Handful per 2 apples | Dried Fruit; apricots; raisins; sultanas |
| 1 | Piece Stem Ginger in syrup | Chopped small |
| 1 | Orange | For the zest |
| 1 tbsp | Icing Sugar | |
| 1 tbsp | Runny Honey | |
| 1 | Pinch Mixed Spice | |
| 1 tsp | Brandy per 2 apples | |

## METHOD
**PREHEAT** oven to 180°C fan
**CORE** Apples
**HEAT** the Butter and Sugar in a small saucepan with the Dried Fruit, Stem Ginger and Orange Zest.
**STIR** until the Butter has melted and all the grains of Sugar have disappeared
**POUR** the mixture into the middle of the Apples, drizzling any extra over the top along with the Honey.
**BAKE** the Apples in the oven for 20 minutes
**MEANWHILE**
**WHIP** the Double Cream with the Icing Sugar and Mixed Spice until you have soft peaks
**FOLD** in the Brandy.
**SERVE** each Apple with a big spoonful of Whipped Cream and any left over Caramel juices.

# EASY & SOME SPECTACULAR

## Plum Pot Pudding

*Well "Pudding" is usually applied to a more stodgy confection so might better be called a "sweet". However, I could not resist the alliteration. It is very good and so very easy, as you will see.*
*Few ingredients; mix them all up and there you are! "Pop" goes the weasel as they say!*

**INGREDIENTS**

| 4 | Ripe Plums | Stoned and sliced |
|---|---|---|
| 100 g | Natural Yoghurt | Low fat or normal – your choice |
| 20 g | Blanched Almonds | |
| 2 tsps | Agave Syrup | |
| 1 | For each glass | Cherry, Strawberry, Grape etc. |

**METHOD**
**CHOOSE** a couple of wide tumblers to serve this sweet
**MIX** the Agave Syrup into the Yoghurt
**PLACE** the slices of one Plum in the bottom of each glass then
**DISTRIBUTE** about half the Yoghurt mixture between the glasses
**PLACE** the remaining Plum slices upright in the glasses.
**POUR** the rest of the Yoghurt into the glasses
**ADD** 1 Cherry; Grape or Strawberry on top in the centre
**SPRINKLE** the Almonds around the top and there you are.

# Caramel & Custard Tart

*Again, a recipe of which the main parts can be cooked in advance up to two days at least. (It does leave your hands relatively free for entertaining!!!). This is delicious especially for a Summer tea in the garden. Do be careful when making the custard and waiting for it to thicken; it takes it's time.*

## INGREDIENTS

| | | |
|---|---|---|
| 3 | Egg Yolks | |
| 85 g | Caster Sugar | |
| 1 tbsp | Plain Flour | |
| 1 tbsp | Corn flour | |
| 250 ml | Skimmed Milk | |
| 1 | Orange | We need the Zest |
| 1 | Egg White | |
| 3 | Sheets Filo Pastry | Each cut in half |
| 3 | Oranges | Skin & pith removed; cut into thin rounds |
| 50 g | Caster Sugar | |

## METHOD

**BEAT** the Egg Yolks with the Sugar until slightly thickened **WHISK** in both Flours

**HEAT** the Milk & Orange Zest in a saucepan

**CATCH** it just before it boils – bubbling at the edges

**WHISK** it into the Egg mix

**POUR** into a heatproof bowl and stand in a larger saucepan with boiling water, **CONSTANTLY STIR** until thickened

**COOL** completely up to two days if necessary.

*When ready*

**PRE-HEAT** oven to 180ᶜC

**BRUSH** Filo Sheets with Egg White and line a 20/23 cm loose bottomed flan tin overlapping the pieces as you go.

**FOLD** the pastry in at the edges so it does not overhang the edge of the tin

**BLIND BAKE** for 10 minutes

**BAKE** for further 5 mins till golden in colour

**LEAVE** to cool – can be 1 day at least

**BEAT** the now cooled Custard mix again until smooth

**SPOON** the mixture into the **CHILL** for at least 30 mins case and

**NOW READY** to serve so **GENTLY HEAT** the Sugar in a non-stick frying pan until Sugar caramelised **SPREAD** the Oranges over the Custard

**DRIZZLE** the caramelised Sugar over the Oranges and leave to set for a couple of minutes

# Peach & Almond Crostata

*This is another, which I picked up in Australia. I have made it twice and was well received so I thought it worth passing on*

**INGREDIENTS**

| 200 g | Ground Almonds | |
|---|---|---|
| 2 tbsp | Coconut Oil | |
| 2 tbsp | Honey | |
| 2 | Eggs | |
| 1 tsp | Vanilla Essence | |
| 2 | Large ripe Peaches | Finely sliced |
| 2 tbsp | Caster Sugar | |
| 1 tbsp | Corn flour | |
| ½ tbsp | Lemon Rind | Buy non-waxed lemon |
| Pinch | Salt | |

**METHOD**

**COMBINE** Salt and Ground Almonds

**MAKE** a well in the middle

**WHISK** Coconut Oil, Honey, I Egg and half the Vanilla

**POUR** into well and **STIR** until dough forms

**WORK** and form a disc

**COVER** in plastic wrap and

**REFRIGERATE** for about an hour

**COMBINE** Peaches, Caster Sugar, Lemon Rind & remaining Vanilla and

**PUT ASIDE** for about fifteen minutes for it to macerate

**PRE-HEAT** Oven to 170°C

**LINE** a large Baking tray with Baking Paper

**SPREAD** Corn flour over the Baking Paper

**REMOVE** dough from fridge and roll out till about 30 cm Square

**WHISK** 2nd Egg

**SPREAD** Peach mixture on the dough leaving about 4 cm clear all around

**FOLD** Dough in to form a rough boundary enclosing the Peaches

**BRUSH** with Whisked Egg

**SPRINKLE** with a little Caster Sugar

**BAKE** for 20 minutes or until the mixture darkens– don't let it go too long at this point

**SERVE** with Ice Cream, Plain Yoghurt or Double Cream or similar. Can be served hot or cold

## Mars Bar Melt

*Now this is something different and if you are trying to impress your daughter or grandchildren this is it. If they fail to be impressed enjoy another glass or two of Prosecco. This is a lush sweet, and I mean sweet, which works very well and has the benefit of being easy to make.*

**INGREDIENTS**

| 4 | Bananas | Peeled and cut into 1 cm chunks |
|---|---|---|
| 40 g | Butter | |
| 20 g | Brown Sugar | |
| 50 g | Salted Roast Peanuts | Crushed |
| Enough | Ice Cream | Vanilla or if you like Chocolate |
| 4 | Mars Bars | Sliced into small chunks |
| 80 ml | Double Cream | |

**METHOD**

**WARM** the Butter with the Brown Sugar

**WHEN** melted add the Bananas

**COOK** until the Bananas are in a slippery state

**PLACE** Bananas into a bowl

**WARM** the chunks of Mars gently in a bowl over simmering water (see illustration below)

**WHEN** the Mars begin to melt

**ADD** the Cream and this will help the melting process, may need a little stirring

**PUT** enough Ice Cream over the Bananas

**COVER** with melted Mars

**TOP** with Peanuts

**SERVE** straightway or put in fridge till wanted but no longer than a couple of hours

# SPECTACULAR

## Crêpe Suzettes

*Now you've seen on the other recipe how to make pancakes let's move on to this simple but showy dish*

**INGREDIENTS**

| 8 | Cooked pancakes | 2 per person |
|---|---|---|
| 50 g | Butter | |
| 25 g | Caster Sugar | |
| 1 tsp | Grated Orange rind | |
| 1 tsp | Grated Lemon Rind | |
| 60 ml | Grand Marnier | Or Cointreau; Curacao |
| 30 ml | Brandy | |

**METHOD**
**FOLD** the pancakes into fan shapes
**MELT** Butter in the frying pan
**ADD** Sugar, Lemon and Orange Rind and Grand Marnier
**BRING** to boil (begins to smell luscious)
**ADD** pancakes 4 will usually fit
**HEAT** through
**TURN** Pancakes twice
**POUR** Brandy into the pan
**SET** alight and allow the flame to die down
**SERVE** as soon as flames have finished
**SECOND** helping with the remaining four pancakes

# Grape Strudel

*This is relatively easy to make but remember to make it with seedless grapes–you really don't want to bother of removing the pips.*
*The Strudel is at its very best when is served chilled with whipped cream. I haven't yet tried but it might even be possible to make it with puff pastry.*

## INGREDIENTS

| 4 sheets | Filo Pastry | At least 30 x 35 cm |
|---|---|---|
| 500 g | Green Seedless Grapes | Red or Black can be used but may need "pipping" |
| 120 g | Butter | Need to melt this early |
| 1 tsp | Ground Cinnamon | |
| | Icing Sugar | To sprinkle over before serving |
| Silicone paper | To line a Baking Tray or Tin | |

## METHOD

**PRE HEAT** OVEN to 200ºC fan
**MELT** Butter in a bowl
**LAY** one sheet of Filo Pastry on the work surface after lightly dusting with Flour
**BRUSH** the Butter all over the Filo Pastry, then
**LAY** another sheet on top of the first and again brush with Butter, and then follow through with two more sheets
**SPREAD** the Grapes over a bit over half of the Pastry starting at one end and allowing space at the edges
**ROLL** the Pastry starting at the end with the Grapes into a salami shape
**TUCK** the edges in before finishing rolling to seal them
**TURN** the strudel over so the seal is underneath – keeps it sealed
**BRUSH** with the remaining Butter
**COOK** for 15 minutes or so until pale golden brown
**SHAKE** a little Icing Sugar over Strudel
**COOL** till ready to serve

# Summer Pudding

*This is a treat and so easy but remember it needs chilling overnight. Which makes it easy to entertain the following day, as there is only one recipe to prepare.*

## INGREDIENTS

| 6 to 8 | Large slices of White Bread | Crusts removed. |
|--------|------------------------------|-----------------|
| 100 g | Sugar | |
| 75 ml | Water | |
| 700 g | Soft Summer fruits – Strawberries, raspberries, stoned cherries, black or red currants | Use as wide a mixture of fruits as you can as it gives a good flavour |
| 150 ml | Double Cream | |
| 15 ml | Fresh Milk | |

## METHOD

**CUT** the Bread into neat fingers

**PUT** Water and Sugar into a saucepan heating slowly till Sugar melts-keep stirring to avoid sticking to pan

**ADD** Fruit and simmer gently for about 7 minutes

**RESERVE** some of the juice

**LINE** a pudding bowl (about 1.1 litre size) with the fingers and cover the bottom with Bread

**ADD** half of the Fruit

**COVER** with more Bread fingers

**ADD** remaining Fruit

**COVER** with more fingers

**PUT** a saucer or plate on top and add a weight on top

**REFRIGERATE** overnight

**TURN** out onto a plate

**COVER** any white spots with the reserved juice

**SERVE** with the Cream whipped lightly with the Milk

**DECORATE** with sprig of Mint

**Excellent so there you are. An alternative is to use Autumnal fruits – blackberries, apples, pears, and plums. All these will need longer simmering**

## Lemon Cheesecake

*OK this is a Cheesecake, which is another recipe I got from Beth in Australia and it really is amazing. You'll just fall in love with it. Cooking is slightly tricky however. It calls for a 'Double Saucepan' – I haven't got one and bet you won't find one in your kitchen – so what to do: simple use a bowl in a saucepan over hot water*

### INGREDIENTS

| | | |
|---|---|---|
| 14 | Chocolate coated biscuits | Chocolate digestive biscuits in England or Chocolate Ripple Biscuits in Australia |
| 50 g | Butter | |
| 60 g | Philadelphia Cream Cheese | |
| 110 g | Sugar | |
| 50 g X 2 | Sugar | Yes two portions |
| 3 | Eggs Yolks | But save the whites you will need them |
| 1 tbsp | Gelatin | |
| ¼ cup | Boiling Water | |
| ¼ cup | Lemon Juice | |
| 100 ml | Double Cream | |

### METHOD
**CRUSH** the Chocolate Biscuits in a large plastic bag beating with a Rolling Pin
**TRANSFER** into a bowl
**MELT** the Butter
**MIX** Butter into the crushed Biscuits
**PRESS** Biscuit mix onto base of a spring form tin Suggest line the tin with Clingfilm first to prevent leakage and difficulty in releasing Cheesecake when ready to serve
**CHILL** in fridge
**COMBINE** Philadelphia Cheese, one portion of Sugar and Egg yolks and
**COOK** in a "double saucepan" (See below) for 10 minutes
**SOAK** 1 tbsp of Gelatin in Lemon Juice
**ADD** ¼ cup Boiling Water and stir till Gelatin is fully dissolved
**STIR** into Cheese/Egg mixture and cool
**BEAT** Egg Whites with the second portion of sugar
**FOLD** into cooled mixture and
**PUT** the whole into the chilled biscuit case
**REFRIGERATE** and decorate with Whipped Cream (double cream beaten till ready)

# Strawberry & Meringue Cheesecake

*This is another Cheesecake and again from Australia – (what is it about Aussies and Cheesecake?) Well whatever it's great and easy to make. It makes enough for 8 servings so good if you are entertaining a number of people. I took the balance round to my son and partner so as not to waste it. Apparently, it wasn't.*

## INGREDIENTS

| 200 g | Sweet Biscuits | Finely chopped in Food Processor |
|-------|----------------|----------------------------------|
| 100 g | Butter | |
| 5 tsp | Powdered Gelatin | |
| 60 ml | Boiling Water | |
| 215 g | Caster Sugar | |
| 750 g | Cream Cheese | At room temperature |
| 1 tsp | Vanilla Extract | |
| 300 ml | Double Cream | |
| 245 g | Strawberry Jam | |
| 4 | Meringues | Chopped |
| 250 g | Fresh Strawberries | Hulled and Halved lengthways |

## METHOD

**GREASE** and line a spring-form tin (if you haven't one you can use a loose bottom flan tin but bear in mind that has less capacity).

**COMBINE** Butter with the Biscuits again using Processor

**PRESS** the Biscuit mixture into the pan

**COOL** in fridge for 30 mins

**POUR** Boiling water into a heatproof bowl

**ADD** Gelatin and **STIR** until dissolved

**LEAVE** to cool, meantime

**BEAT** Cream, Cheese, and Sugar & Vanilla until smooth

**BEAT** in the cooled Gelatin

**FOLD** in cream mixture and **STIR IN** Strawberry jam

**SPOON** filling over the prepared base

**COVER** and place in fridge overnight to set

**TRANSFER** Cheesecake to serving plate

**PILE** Strawberries & Meringue Chunks on top

**SLICE & SERVE**

Just lovely I could do with a serving just now!

# Christmas Pudding

*Go on just try this and surprise everybody. We cook this in the microwave so does not take hours and hours steaming the usual way. Makes enough for 8 anyway. Now you need to "rub-in" so see how in the Techniques section*

## INGREDIENTS

| 60 g | Plain Flour | |
|------|-------------|---|
| 150 g | Butter | |
| ½ tsp | Mixed Spice | |
| ½ tsp | Ground Nutmeg | |
| 110 g | Fresh Breadcrumbs | |
| 110 g | Dark Brown Sugar | Ordinary Brown Sugar will suffice |
| 100 g | Raisins | |
| 100 g | Sultanas | |
| 25 g | Chopped Mixed Peel | |
| 25 g | Blanched Almonds chopped | Or Walnut halves |
| 1 | Orange | Needed for Rind |
| 2 | Eggs | Beaten |
| 30 ml | Brandy | Or Sherry |
| ½ tsp | Almond Essence | |

## METHOD

**CUT** the Butter into the Flour with a rounded knife then

**RUB-IN** as described in the Techniques section using a large bowl

**ADD** Breadcrumbs, Sugar, Raisins, Sultanas, Peel, Nuts, Orange Rind, Nutmeg and Mixed Spice

**MIX WELL**

**COMBINE** with Eggs, Brandy, Almond Essence and Milk **MIX WELL** again

**GREASE** 1 litre pudding basin

**FILL** the basin to the top

**COVER** with greaseproof paper and leave sufficient room for pudding to rise.

**SECURE** paper with a rubber band or string

**ADJUST** microwave power setting to 30% (not all microwaves act in the same way so ensure you know how to adjust power on your microwave cooker)

**COOK** for 25-30 minutes.

It is ready to eat straightaway or can wait for weeks until ready – in the latter case ensure it remains covered. From time to time if you like you can add a teaspoon of brandy letting it soak through but not too much.

# CAKES (Just in case)

## Fruit Loaf Cake

*This is an easy to make fruit cake – beloved by grandchildren (and others). I've made it for charity events – to eat and to raffle as a prize. So have a go with this one*

**INGREDIENTS**

| 200 g | Self-raising flour | |
|-------|--------------------|--|
| Pinch | Salt | |
| 1 tsp | Mixed Spice | |
| 100 g | Butter | |
| 100 g | Sugar | |
| 575 g | Mixed Fruit | |
| 110 ml | Milk | Might need a touch more |
| 1 | Egg | Lightly beaten |
| 50 g | Demerara Sugar | For Topping before baking |

**METHOD**
**STIR** Flour, Salt and Mixed Spice into a bowl –big enough for a kilo of mixture
**RUB IN** Butter (as shown in Techniques section)
**ADD** Sugar and Fruit
**BEAT** Egg into Milk
**ADD** to mixture
**STIR** mixture thoroughly (may need a little more Milk if stiff) should "drop" from spoon
**SPOON** into tin either lined with baking paper or a bought liner from a kitchen shop  (for example in England - Lakeland) saves a lot of fuss especially when taking cake from tin to cool and rest.
**SPRINKLE** Demerara Sugar over top
**BAKE** at 160°C for 1 hr. 40 mins

**TEST** after 1 & 1/2 hours. Cake should be smelling very nice! And be a darkish golden brown colour. Insert a skewer and if it comes out clean the cake is done. If any mixture is on the skewer then cook for a further 15 mins.
If the cake appears to be over browning after an hour cover with tin foil – I always do this anyway.

# Dundee Cake

*This cake is great. Be quick though Scotland has applied to the EU for protected status. If granted before Brexit - then can only be made in Scotland. It takes concentration for the decoration. On the other hand, it is a particularly delicious cake. I've described how to line the tin but it is possible to buy ready-made liners which save time and effort. In England Lakeland is the shop to go to for this (also on online).*

## INGREDIENTS

| | | |
|---|---|---|
| 175 g | Butter | Plus a little to melt and grease tin |
| 175 g | Caster Sugar | |
| 3 | Eggs | |
| 225 g | Plain Flour | |
| 50 g | Ground Almonds | |
| 100 g | Currants | |
| 100 g | Sultanas | |
| 100 g | Raisins | |
| 50 g | Chopped Mixed Peel | |
| 30 ml | Fresh Milk | |
| 100 g | Blanched & Split Almonds | |
| 1 ½ tsp | Baking powder | |

## METHOD

**CUT OUT**, from baking parchment, shapes to cover all sides of a 20 cm tin

**GREASE** with melted Butter the inside and base of tin then line with the shapes and grease the parchment as well.

**RUB-IN** Butter and Sugar until light and fluffy. You need to build as much air into the mixture at this stage

**BEAT** in Eggs one at a time adding 1 tablespoon of the Flour with each

**ADD** Currants, Sultanas, Raisins and Mixed Peel

**ADD** Milk with I tablespoon of Flour

**SIEVE** remaining Flour with the Baking Powder and gently

**FOLD** in with a large metal spoon

**TRANSFER** to the prepared tin and smooth the top with a knife

**COVER** the top with the Split Almonds

**BAKE** at 150ºC fan for 2 ½ to 3 hours – at least till a skewer comes out clean

**LEAVE** in tin for 5/6 minutes

**TURN** out onto a wire cooling rack

**CAREFULLY** peel off the paper when cake is cold.

**Store in an airtight container and the cake will last for a long time.**
**What I do is to cut it into slices and wrap individually in cling film and freeze. You then have a good cake ready for use when unexpected visitors arrive.**

# Biscuits

*This is simple and takes little time. My daughter is allowing me to show my 5-year-old Granddaughter this recipe. Should produce some good Grandfather points when I get around to it (she lives in  Australia.)*

## INGREDIENTS– makes about 12 biscuits

| | | |
|---|---|---|
| 150 g | Plain Flour | |
| ½ Cup | Caster Sugar | |
| 100 g | Butter | |
| 1 Cup | Rolled Oats | |
| 2 tbsp | Golden Syrup | |
| 1 tsp | Baking Soda | |
| 1 tsp | Vanilla Extract | |
| 1 tsp | Cinnamon | Not important if you don't like this flavour |
| 1 tbsp | Boiling Water | |
| 2 | Baking Trays | Cover with Baking Parchment. Keep after as will serve at least for a dozen more 'cookings' |

## METHOD

**PREHEAT** oven on fan bake to 180$^0$C fan

**COVER** 2 baking trays with baking parchment.

**MIX** Flour, Sugar, Oats and (if using) Cinnamon in a bowl until well combined

**MELT** Butter and Syrup – 1 minute in microwave does that very well

**COMBINE** the Boiling Water with the Baking Soda and Vanilla Essence

**ADD** to Butter mixture ensuring that all Butter is melted

**MIX** Oats and Butter mixtures together to make Dough

**DROP** tablespoonfuls of the Dough onto the baking trays.

**MAKE** into pyramids or domes and

**FLATTEN** each one gently

**LEAVE** sufficient space between each for them to spread of about 2 1/2 – 3 cm

**BAKE** for about 10 minutes or until edges become golden.

**TURN** baking tray around if not golden and

**BAKE** for a further 3 minutes

**STAND** for about 4/5 minutes on cooling rack to become cool and crisp

**SAVE** in Biscuit Tin so they do not become hard.

I find these very useful in that mid-morning and midafternoon one of these biscuits and a cup of tea give the blood sugar a boost until the next meal without a feeling of hunger. This is purely personal but it certainly helps weight control.

**ENJOY!**

# Scones

*Scones are simple and there are three versions but the principles are the same. The only differences are what you put in so here are the ingredients for each. Also, bearing in mind my belief that buying a ready-made product might be quicker and as good as doing the whole job yourself, I can recommend Paul Hollywood's Ready Made Scone Mix. This will only replace the "sifting flour and salt into a bowl" step below. You will still need to rub in. (See in Techniques section Part Three). But try it.*

**INGREDIENTS**

| 225 g | Self-Raising Flour | |
|---|---|---|
| 50 g | Butter | |
| 150 ml | Fresh Milk | |
| 60 g | Cheese | Grated |
| 2/3 | Spring Onions | Finely chopped |
| 15 g | Parmesan Cheese | |
| 1 tsp | Ready-made Mustard | |
| 1 tsp | Cayenne Pepper | |
| 25 g | Sultanas | Or Mixed Fruit |
| 1 | Medium Egg | |
| ½ tsp | Salt | |

**METHOD**

**PRE-HEAT** oven to 230ºC fan

**LINE** a baking tray with Parchment

**SIFT** Flour and Salt into a bowl

**RUB-IN** Butter into Flour mix (see in Techniques video 'Rubbing-in ')

**ADD** Grated Cheese, Cayenne Pepper and Spring Onions *–for Cheese Scones*]

[**ADD** Sultanas or Mixed Fruit *for fruit scones*]

**STIR** Mustard into Milk *if making Cheese scones* or just

**ADD** Milk

**MIX** to a slightly soft Dough with a knife

**PREPARE** a Floured surface and

**TURN** the mixture onto the Floured surface and knead quickly (Flour your hand while doing this) until quite smooth

**PAT** out so the Dough is about 2 cm thick

**CUT** into scone shapes with a biscuit cutter about 6/7 cm in diameter

**TRANSFER** the Scone onto the baking tray

**BRUSH** tops with Milk

**SPRINKLE** with Parmesan Cheese *for Cheese Scones*

**BAKE** for about 7 – 10 minutes or until the Scones are well risen and golden in colour

**COOL** on a wire cooling rack

**SERVE** Fruit Scones with Clotted Cream and Strawberry Jam.

**They do freeze well – but remember to cut in half first**

## Scrambled Eggs

*Now here are two ways to scramble eggs, neither is better than the other it is what you prefer doing that counts*

### INGREDIENTS

| | | |
|---|---|---|
| 2 | Free Range Eggs | |
| 30 ml | Milk; Single or Double Cream or Water | |
| 15 g | Butter | Soft preferable |
| | Salt & Pepper | To taste |

### METHOD 1 On the Hob

**WHISK** the Eggs, Cream; Water or Milk pinch of Salt until nicely combined
**HEAT** the Butter in a non-stick frying pan
**MAKE** sure the butter doesn't brown
**POUR** in the egg mixture
**LET it** sit for about 20 seconds without stirring then
**STIR** with a wooden spoon lifting and folding it over from the bottom of the pan
**LET** it sit again for 10 seconds
**REPEAT** until eggs are set – doesn't matter if slightly runny in places
**REMOVE** from heat and leave for 5/6 seconds to finish cooking
**FINAL** stir then serve

### METHOD 2 Microwave

**WHISK** Eggs as before in a large bowl
**ADD** Milk or Cream or Water and Butter; Salt & Pepper for seasoning
**MICROWAVE** on 50% power (see below) for 2 minutes
**REMOVE** and stir in around the edges, which should just be beginning to cook
**MICROWAVE** again but only for 1 minute
**REMOVE** and stir gain
**REPEAT** until Eggs are cooked and scrambled to your liking

*Cooking at reduced power level.*
*Dial up time required*
*Press "Power level" button until the required % shows – for eggs 50%*
*Press "Start/Cook"*

## Ham in Cider

*This is the way to make flavoursome ham, which you can use in cooking (Murphy Casserole) or in sandwiches. If you are in England M & S do an extremely good joint which responds to this treatment. If you are elsewhere you need to find a joint prepared in the way English butchers do. In Australia I found an English butcher in Dandenong Victoria – But if you are in Cairns or Perth that is no help but maybe someone out there knows! Meantime here goes.*

**INGREDIENTS**

| 1 kg | Ham Joint | |
|------|-----------|--|
| 1.5 litres | Cider | Personal choice – Strongbow works for me |
| 4 | Cloves | |
| 1 | Medium Onion | Cut in half |
| 1 | Bouquet Garni | |
| 75 g | Carrots | Sliced lengthwise |
| 1 stick | Celery | Sliced lengthwise |
| 6 | Juniper berries | Not easy to find but see Techniques section for alternatives |
| 6 | Black Peppercorns | |

**METHOD**
**PLACE** Ham joint in a large saucepan, cover with water and bring to boil
**DRAIN** and **RINSE** foam from joint
**CLEAN** the pan
**RETURN** Ham joint to pan and **ADD** Cider – use enough to cover the joint to save adding water but ensure joint is covered.
**PUSH** 2 Cloves into each Onion half, and then **ADD** them to the pan with Bouquet Garni, Carrots, Celery, Juniper Berries and Peppercorns.
**BRING** to the boil then
**LOWER** heat and simmer for 1hr 15 minutes *Take care not to cook it any longer or it will become tough and dry.*
**REMOVE** from pan; discard the cooking liquid and flavourings and leave to stand for about 15 minutes
**TRIM** away any fat then carve the meat into slices and serve
**NOTE** If you are going to serve cold leave to cool in the cooking liquid as this keeps meat succulent

## White Sauce - Roux

**INGREDIENTS**

| 30 g | Plain flour | |
|------|-------------|---|
| 20 g | Butter | |
| 125 ml | Milk | |
| Touch | Salt | |
| ½ tsp | Black Pepper | |
| ½ tsp | Mustard | Ready made |

**METHOD**
**MELT** Butter in saucepan
**ADD** Flour then
**WHISK** Flour gradually into the Cold milk
**HEAT** for 2 minutes whisking slowly all the time
**ADD** Salt, Pepper, Mustard mixed in a little water
**SIMMER** very slowly (low heat) for about 5 minutes till thickens. Don't let it become too thick.

**Flavours**
**Parsley Sauce** add one heaped finely chopped Parsley to the cooked sauce
**Cheese sauce** stir 100 g of grated Cheese into sauce
**Onion Sauce** Peel, chop, and fry one Onion until tender. Stir into cooked sauce.

**For a Gluten free sauce**
**SUBSTITUTE** 15 g Corn flour for the Plain Flour and proceed as above. This gets thick and gloppy very fast so you may need to add more Milk. For larger quantities use same proportions (15 g Corn flour to each 125 ml Milk)

## Cooking Rice

**DECIDE**  how much Rice to cook. The best proportions of Rice to water are 1 cup rice to 1.75 cups of water. (2 cups are plenty for 4 servings)

**MEASURE**  amount of water you are going to need.
Use a **large** saucepan with a tight fitting lid

**BOIL**  water and add 1 teaspoon salt

**ADD**  Rice to boiling water

**STIR**  once, or just enough to separate Rice

Use wooden spoon to separate any clumps.
**Don't over stir**. That can cause the Rice to become sticky.

**COVER**  the pot and simmer

Be sure that the lid fits tightly on the pot. Turn down the heat to its lowest setting  (2 works here).
Let rice simmer for about 18 minutes. Then remove from heat and allow the Rice to simmer in the pot for another five minutes.

**FLUFF**  Rice with a fork

Just before serving gently fluff the Rice to separate the grains.

**TIP**

**Don't uncover the saucepan or stir the Rice during cooking**.  If it's done before you're ready to serve it, place a folded tea towel over the saucepan, replace the lid and set aside. The towel will absorb excess moisture and condensation helping prevent overcooked and mushy Rice.

## Rubbing – in

From time to time you will need to "rub – in" for a recipe. Usually this is when making Pastry, which of course you won't do with my recipes – you buy it in.

But it is sometimes needed for other recipes such as Fruit Crumble.

So, let's do it

I find it a calming task; great thinking time and quite enjoy the process

You need hard butter, i.e. from the fridge - not soft spreading butter.

Cut the butter into small pieces or cubes – but not too big
Put it into a bowl with the flour and mix up the butter until it is all coated with flour.

With your fingertips pick up small amounts of the mixed butter/flour and rub them together using your thumbs to rub from small finger to first finger.

Do make sure you raise your hand well above the mixture as we are trying not to heat the mixture but to keep the butter cool whilst the process carries on – we do not want it to soften.

If you feel it is beginning to soften then place the bowl into the fridge for 10/15 mins (Coffee break-time!).

Keep rubbing in and the mixture will begin to look like breadcrumbs – nearly there.

Just shake the bowl gently to see if there are any lumps still in the mixture – keep on rubbing till there are none.

## Chopping Onions

It occurred to me that many of the recipes have onions in them and whilst you a busily chopping them or whatever the recipe demands you might well have suffered from the gas (which is a mild form of sulphuric acid) released when an
onion is cut making the eyes water and also sting.

## No Longer!!!!

To avoid this unpleasantness chill the onions for 30/45 minutes before you start preparation. Better still is keep them in the fridge anyway

## However

If you have not had time to put them in the fridge just wipe the cutting board with white vinegar

Happy cooking!

# Herbs & Spices Substitution

*The time comes when a recipe demands a herb or spice and you haven't got it in the Pantry. This always happens at the last minute and there is no time to go to the store – perhaps you are halfway through preparing the recipe…HELP!!! Below is a rudimentary list of possible substitutions, which may relieve the situation. Some are stronger than others so be careful but this is an emergency.*

*These lists are not definitive but just those I've needed or looked up for the purpose of this Post*

| Herb | Possible substitutes |
|---|---|
| Basil | Marjoram, Mint, Oregano, Rosemary, Savory or Thyme |
| Chervil | Cilantro, Parsley or Tarragon |
| Cilantro | Chervil, Parsley, or Tarragon |
| Juniper berries | Rosemary, Cardamom, Ginger or teaspoon of Gin per 4 berries required |
| Chive | Leek or Onion |
| Marjoram | Basil, Mint, or Thyme |
| Mint | Basil, Marjoram or Rosemary |
| Oregano | Basil or Thyme |
| Parsley | Chervil or Cilantro |
| Rosemary | Mint, Rosemary, Tarragon or Thyme |
| Sage | Marjoram, Rosemary, Tarragon or Thyme |
| Tarragon | Chervil or Rosemary |
| Thyme | Basil, Marjoram, or Oregano |

| Spice | Possible substitutes |
|---|---|
| Allspice | Cinnamon, Cloves or Mace |
| Aniseed | Fennel seed |
| Cardamom | Ginger |
| Cloves | Allspice, Cinnamon or Nutmeg |
| Cinnamon | Allspice, Mace or Nutmeg |
| Ginger | Allspice, Cinnamon, Mace or Nutmeg |
| Mace | Allspice, Cinnamon, Ginger or Nutmeg |
| Paprika | Cayenne Pepper |
| Nutmeg | Cinnamon, Cloves, Ginger or Mace |
| Saffron | Annatto or Turmeric |
| Turmeric | Annatto or Saffron |

**Allspice is a bit ubiquitous on the list (probably why I found it in the larder in a bigger container than the others). My experience is that it is stronger than some of the others so tend to reduce amount when using as a substitute.**

Printed in Great Britain
by Amazon